ISBN: 979-8-9944073-0-1

Printed and bound in NYC

Copyright © 2026 by Pia Silva.

Book and Cover design by Steve Wasterval

All rights reserved. Printed in the United States of America. No part of this book may be used or reproduced in any manner whatsoever

without written permission except in the case of brief quotations embodied in critical articles or reviews.

Limit of Liability/Disclaimer of Warranty: While the publisher and author have used their best efforts in preparing this book, they make no representations or warranties with respect to the accuracy or completeness of the contents of this book and specifically disclaim any implied warranties of merchantability or fitness for a particular purpose.

No warranty may be created or extended by sales representatives or written sales materials. The advice and strategies contained herein may not be suitable for your situation. You should consult with a professional where appropriate. The author shall not be liable for any loss of profit or any other commercial damages, including but not limited to special, incidental, consequential, or other damages.

For information contact;

Worstofall Design LLC

37 Greenpoint Ave

Brooklyn, NY 11222

www.nobsmastery.com

ISBN: 979-8-9944073-0-1

First Edition: March 2026

Printed in the United States of America

10 9 8 7 6 5 4 3 2 1

SCALE SOLO

PIA SILVA

TABLE OF CONTENTS

INTRODUCTION	
PART ONE: THE NO BS BUSINESS MODEL	01
PART TWO: NO BS MARKETING	31
PART THREE: NO BS SALES	89
PART FOUR: NO BS DELIVERY	143
PART FIVE: NO BS MONEY MINDSET	203
CONCLUSION	245
ACKNOWLEDGMENTS	255

INTRODUCTION

You didn't start your business to drown in client drama or chase payments.

You also didn't start it to build a massive team and chase endless growth.

You started it for freedom—more time and flexibility, less hassle and working for the man, and real autonomy.

When I wrote *Badass Your Brand*, my goal was to inspire people to own their uniqueness and not be afraid to stand out and be seen as the badasses they are. In the process, I told our story about how we clawed our way out of debt and built a tiny, profitable, nimble branding business that didn't run our lives.

I thought the book would be a helpful behind-the-scenes guide for entrepreneurs who were struggling to stand out in a crowded world.

But something unexpected happened: people all over the world started asking me to teach them how I ran *our* business. Designers, copywriters, coaches, marketers, consultants—they were all tired of hustling for clients, drowning in client bullshit, and feeling like glorified freelancers.

The book didn't just inspire them to rethink their brands.

They wanted the full playbook on *my* business.

"I love the idea of selling the first step instead of pitching for free, but how do I do that?"

"How can you possibly deliver so much in such a short amount of time, and how can I do that without sacrificing value?"

"How can I get booked out *months* in advance?"

These were all new ideas to them, and they questioned whether it was even possible. Was this just some magic that only Pia and Steve could deliver? Or was this a repeatable model that was *really possible* for them?

If it was, they wanted in.

But the thing I heard most was this: "Thank you for showing me that it's possible to have the business and life I want without hiring a big team."

People wanted to learn more about my methods because we found success while staying intentionally small.

I heard from so many people who, like me, weren't trying to build a huge business or make millions. They were grateful I wasn't pushing them to hire, because they wanted what I wanted: to earn more in less time, reliably, on their own.

What they really needed was *permission*—and a playbook.

So in 2021, I decided to start a new business to teach our whole method, end-to-end.

The one that allowed us to earn $250,000–$500,000 a year while working with clients less than 50% of our time. The one that gave us the freedom to do a few projects one month, then travel without work for the next three. The one that gave me the flexibility to forgo client work for *months* to write and publish my first book.

I knew some of my methods could work for others since I

had already been installing them in my private brand clients' businesses for years.

But the real breakthrough came when I realized the clutter and chaos—mental, operational, and strategic—had been the thieves robbing me of that freedom, and were likely the culprit for other business owners as well.

The overwhelming noise of endless "should-dos" driven by vague goals and the default business model that turns projects into chaos. It's the marketing grind that promises everything, takes everything *out* of you, and delivers little, if anything, in return.

Your business starts to feel like a junk drawer full of half-implemented systems, random marketing tactics, and advice pieced together from dozens of Instagram gurus and business books. You're exhausted from trying to do it all, but terrified of skipping the *one thing* that might *actually* work.

This has been the plight of small businesses for as long as I've been working for myself (in 20 years, I've never had a "real" job!). And the rapid advances in technology—tech that was supposed to make things easier—have only made it worse.

As technology advances at an exponential pace, so does the pressure to do more, faster, and all at once.

You wake up with a running list of "shoulds" before you even check your phone: the marketing tactics you are not doing, the systems you haven't built, the team you think you're *supposed* to hire. It all swirls around you, a constant hum of guilt and overwhelm.

Then you open your computer and the forty browser tabs

you left open the night before stare back at you, each one a reminder of another thing you forgot to worry about. This clutter isn't harmless; it's actively robbing you of the very freedom you started this business to create.

That's where this book steps in.

I want to show you a business model that will remove the overwhelm and replace it with a simple, proven system.

I've broken the book up into five sections that will give you the complete picture of what your business can look like if you strip away the chaos and just focus on the few things that support the goals of freedom and ease:

- A **financial model** based on the 50/25/25 Rule to Profit and Freedom that balances work and growth (and lets you know when you've done *enough*… with numbers!)
- A **marketing model** that focuses on a few consistent actions to keep your pipeline filled with prospects, and allows you to get rid of all the other marketing-related "shoulds."
- A **sales model** that uses The Lead Product™ Method to replace free pitches (positioning you as a high-value authority and saving you a boatload of time).
- A **delivery model** built around Intensives, which deliver more value in a shorter timeline—a win-win for you and your clients.
- A **money mindset model** with a cash flow strategy that I believe is necessary to achieve freedom and ease.

Use this business model as the backbone of a business that serves your life, not the other way around.

My journey from debt to a lean $360,000 operation on half-time proves it, and so do the hundreds of students who've turned my methods into their own wins.

Students who:
- walked away from draining retainer clients that made them feel underappreciated and constantly on call;
- booked out months ahead with boundaried projects that let them have clients on the books *and* check-out, rest, and vacation without their laptop in between;
- closed their highest-priced projects ever (often with clients who originally told them their budget was *half* that) with ease;
- shifted their mindset to charge more for a project that takes less time to deliver, and believe that it's worth it;
- and, most importantly… claimed **real freedom over their time.**

Think of this book—and the stories of real people who have done this that you'll encounter throughout—as your permission slip to stop trying to grow just because you think you're *supposed to*, or because that's what a "real" business looks like.

Instead, start building a freedom-first, lifestyle-focused business that acts like a cash register to fund the parts of your life that matter most, while allowing you to do fulfilling, valuable work that excites you.

You'll shift your perspective on what running a business can look like *in reality*, rather than in polished reels on Instagram, and get inspired to take intentional action.

For People Who Chose Freedom On Purpose

I'm pretty sick of the following rhetoric that gets lobbed at solo owners like grenades:

"If you don't have an assistant, you *are* the assistant."

"If you're doing the work, you don't own a business—you own a job."

"Real entrepreneurs scale with a team."

I get the sentiment, and I've even said some of those things, too. But I think they do real harm, and fill our heads with unnecessary "shoulds." They disparage an entire group of super-smart and talented people—the ones who chose self-employment because they wanted agency over their lives, enjoy their craft, and care deeply about their family, friends, and freedom.

They relegate us to a second-class category: "Not *real* business owners."

I disagree.

Over the past 15 years, I've built multiple businesses while also coaching and consulting hundreds of people from this savvy group. On that journey, I've met so many enthusiastic and skilled people who went out on their own—not with dreams of making millions, but simply to own their life, their way. They want to pick clients they like, protect their time, and do meaningful, *enjoyable* work. And the idea of hiring a big team of employees—and all the overhead and management that comes with that—just doesn't appeal to them. Like, *at all*.

They want lean, and they want *flexible*. They want ease, peace, and security. They want respect for their work, they want freedom, and they want *enough*.

And they want to be respected for that choice, too.

If you're feeling compelled to raise your fist with a "hell yeah!"...

This book is for you.

I know you because *I am you.* Flexibility and freedom have been my drivers since the day I graduated from college and chose not to apply for jobs like everyone else. I had exactly one "real" job for a few months before I realized I would rather hustle 24/7 than have to report to *anyone* at 9am on a Monday.

I "gigged" before that was a term, cobbling together enough to live on from bartending, trying to sell real estate, and "consulting" for various startups (which basically just meant I was paid to help them figure out how to launch). I hustled *hard,* and I didn't mind too much! As long as I wasn't working for "the man," I was happy enough.

Then I met Steve—talented, chatty, and full of just enough enthusiasm to follow my wild ideas. I saw an uber-talented man that I loved, but when it came to the money and management side of things, there was a lot left to be desired. And I thought, *I'm the exact kind of spreadsheet-loving, figure-it-out type of gal that could make this work.*

That's when we decided to go all in on building our branding agency, Worstofall Design, together. I told Steve I'd free him up to focus on what he was best at—designing—and I'd do the rest.

How? I had no idea!

I knew nothing about design, had never set foot in the agency world, and my entrepreneurial background was completely informed by my gig years. But I had heart and a fierce determination to "make it work," which literally just meant getting by without having to fall back on bartending.

I made a lot of mistakes while figuring it out. This book is the guide I wish I'd had. And now it's yours.

Who This Book Is (and Isn't) For

If your greatest asset right now is your **skill**—your ability to deliver a valuable service—this is your playbook. If you want to earn great money, love your work, and keep your calendar humane, this is your model.

If you're building a funded tech startup or you're obsessed with headcount and hockey-stick growth, you will not like this book. That's okay, because there are a thousand other books written for you. This one is for everyone else—the significantly larger group that simply wants autonomy, excellence, and a beautiful life.

That said, if you sell your expert services and *eventually* want a bigger company—or have future dreams of passive income products—this model can still serve you. I used it to generate cash, develop skills, and bank confidence, all of which helped me build both real and perceived authority. I also used it to fund the next business, using the profits and time it generated, because those other business models require a runway to succeed.

While I now run a scalable business with a team, overhead, and bigger financial goals, I've been able to do it profitably—without compromising my lifestyle or time with my young child (you can't get these years back!)—because I built it on **The No BS Business Model** I share in this book. This approach lets me earn more while protecting my time, stability, and priorities.

Because this book is not anti-growth, it's anti-**unintentional** growth.

It's pro-model—a business model for expert-led service businesses seeking to stay small and profitable without hiring a team.

I call it the *No BS* Business Model because it cuts out the superfluous nonsense that wastes your time, eats up your profit, erodes your life, and even devalues your work. This model streamlines your business so you can focus on what matters most: serving clients, maintaining profitability, and enjoying your life outside of work. Built by an impatient New Yorker (hi!) who hates inefficiency and wasted time.

If you're going to spend your one wild life building something, why not go for the gold? Why not aim to hit every goal for you *and* your clients? As a recovering perfectionist, I'm learning to balance wanting everything to be outstanding with accepting that nothing is perfect (though we can try!). My business goal is to meet my highest expectations without being paralyzed by them, and to be recognized when the work is great.

If you're nodding along, you're my people.

Last warning: I'm going to say things you haven't heard before. Sure, I know people say that all the time. But this book contains ideas that are completely opposite to what many tout. Frankly, I'm a little nervous to share them.

There are also radical ideas in here that will make some people bristle if they are set on staying in a certain mindset. For example, some things I suggest will sound impossible (they're not). Or you might draw the wrong conclusions, like I'm suggesting you pressure people (I'm not). Or your existing mindset might lead you to think I'm telling you to do things like go into debt (I'm definitely not).

I think the reason other people aren't saying these things out loud is that they're worried about telling people to do things they can't do, and then not wanting to be responsible if they don't do them correctly.

But you're all adults. I trust you to use the powerful strategies I'm about to teach you responsibly.

I encourage you to read with a beginner's mindset. Instead of rejecting ideas due to immediate aversion, suspend your beliefs as you read and consider that what I say may well be possible for you.

Let's get to it!

PART ONE

The No BS Business Model

Playing it back in my head feels like those classic horror movies where the female lead is happily whistling to herself while she gets ready for a shower, blissfully unaware of the crazy ax murderer lurking just behind the door.

That was me in 2012—poor, naive 28-year-old Pia, belting out Gotye's "Somebody That I Used to Know" without a care in the world, riding high on enthusiasm. We had just landed what seemed like the perfect client: a small consulting firm that needed "a new brand and website," exactly the kind of end-to-end project that we wanted (and needed for our portfolio).

We were going to blow this project out of the water. More clients with similar projects were surely out there, ready to hire us once we could show them we could handle making their entire business stand out with a badass brand.

I was thrilled when they (finally) accepted our proposal.

As soon as we got the green light, I dove in, unaware I'd already made my first mistakes—and I was soon going to pay for it dearly.

The client was three partners who, in retrospect, had vastly different ideas of what they wanted, where they were going, and what they had hired us to do.

I didn't see that yet, of course.

In hindsight, the problems started on the first call—eager-beaver me saying yes to everything, noting their website needs, pages, and extras, promising a proposal soon.

By this point, our proposals had grown from a single-page Word document to a full 25-page deck detailing our capabilities, carefully selected example designs to match their taste, and lots of pretty pages, each one unfolding the story of why we were a perfect match for them. Then came the lengthy list of deliverables, along with a long, detailed timeline (complete with calendar graphics), every detail bulked up so I could justify the price.

The price was high, but they needed a lot. When I estimated the number of hours it would take and multiplied it by our hourly rate, it came out to almost $10,000. Since I didn't think they would pay that (and I had never charged one client that much at once), I set the price at an uncomfortable but not totally inconceivable $8,500, still the most we had ever charged for a single project.

At first, I thought they ghosted us once they saw the price, since I didn't hear *anything* back for a few weeks. When they finally answered the 4th follow-up, they said they were still interested, but it was more than they had hoped to spend. Could we do it for around $7,000? And also, they needed a brochure designed. Could we *just* add that in as well?

Three more phone meetings with the partners and a dozen emails going over the details in the deliverables list and verbiage in the contract, and we finally agreed on a $7,250 project, with everything they asked for, but with the promise of more work after.

When we finally had a signed contract and a promise that the check was "going in the mail today," we celebrated with some "Three Buck Chuck" at home. We were tired, but excited to finally get to work—the fun part!

I could fill this whole book with the details of how this project unfolded, but I don't want to give you PTSD. Because if you're reading this—and you work on projects with multiple deliverables and clients—I know you already know *exactly* what I'm talking about.

"We really love a few of these options, but none of them are quite it. What else have you got?"

Each round of designs presented was met with both praise and endless opinions. First, they liked the logo options, but none of them were *quite right,* and they wanted us to explore more ideas. Then they weren't sure if they wanted a rebrand after all—maybe just "refresh the old one." We dutifully followed every request to move things along and get to the next payment.

Each phase that was intended to take weeks turned into months, with additional rounds of revisions, meetings, and gaps of time when we were just waiting on the edge of our seats for their feedback.

When one partner wanted it sleeker, another wanted it friendlier, and the third just wanted it to "pop" more. Nothing was ever good enough, but everything was "close… almost there."

Meanwhile, the hours we had budgeted evaporated. I answered each new email as quickly as possible, at all hours of the day and night, imagining that if we could just get <current step> approved, maybe it would get easier.

By the time the project limped across the finish line, Steve and I were exhausted and frustrated. When I had to follow up five times on the final check that had supposedly been mailed but never arrived, weeks after the project was finished and the website was live, I was questioning whether I had the stomach for this line of work. When I looked back and calculated how many hours we spent on this project, we made $20/hour, $10/hour less than Steve was making at the low-paying freelance job he had right before we started working for ourselves.

What I know now that I wish I'd known then: It *wasn't* that I wasn't cut out for it. **It was that the way we were working was *causing* the chaos because it was *inherently broken*.**

The Default Model

While that was a particularly egregious case, elements of it crept into every project we did in those early years running our small branding agency, Worstofall Design.

And I was always looking for someone to blame. Was there something wrong with me? Do "clients just suck," and were we magnets for impossible-to-please personalities?

Both were hard to stomach because while they were driving us crazy, these clients almost always *liked* us a lot, including at the end of the projects! They were thankful, happy with the final product, often wanted to take us out for a drink after, and even referred us to others. And as people, I liked them too. While I wished they would just *make a freakin' decision,* I could also empathize with them wanting to love it.

I now know that what happened with those early clients wasn't their fault. *Every* client became a challenge *because my process was messy.* There were just too many opportunities for it to go sideways.

I was running my business in the Default Model—the same hamster wheel most experts selling their services get trapped on.

The Default Model includes some or all of the following:

- **Free work up front.** Hours of unpaid planning, meetings, and advice to "win" the work.
- **Hourly or vague pricing.** Projects are paid by the hour, or based on an hourly estimate.
- **Built-in obstacles for momentum.** Payments are tied to project phases that are largely reliant on the client taking action.
- **Client as boss.** You say yes to everything and jump to meet every request because you're afraid of upsetting the client or losing the work.
- **Scope creep, endless revisions, or change requests.** Projects stretch on for months longer than they should, eating into your profit and sanity. And/or clients become a constant stream of requests and emails.

- **Retainers as a band-aid.** You tack on a monthly fee, hoping for stability, but end up at their beck and call.

I learned the Default Model by copying all the other small agencies I met while networking. It seemed like this was the *only* way to run this business since everyone I met was doing it this way.

But the school of hard knocks taught me this: **the Default Model *guarantees* you'll stay overworked and underpaid if you are selling your services directly to clients.**

The Default Model keeps you in survival mode because there are too many moving parts for one or two people to handle with ease. You get stuck swinging between feast and famine because you oscillate between months of delivering underpriced work, followed by panic and spaghetti-at-the-wall marketing efforts when the pipeline dries up.

You never get ahead because you're too busy serving clients to build a sustainable business foundation that would solve the problem long term.

No wonder so many small service businesses burn out.

Luckily, I found a better way. But I had to go through some pain to get there.

The Failure That Changed Everything

My first book, *Badass Your Brand*, opens with the story of us being $40,000 in debt and then making $500,000 in the following 12 months. Just the two of us. That story is completely true. But I could tell that same story very differently by adding one more number.

In March of 2014, *we had generated $250,000 in revenue over the previous twelve months and were still $40,000 in debt.*

Same facts. Completely different framing.

The reason we were in debt wasn't just that we couldn't find enough clients. *It was because our projects were not profitable.*

Here's how I figured it out:

At first, I had no idea what I was doing wrong. To get clients, we spent weeks doing things we saw other agencies do, like creating fancy decks and shooting cool promo videos.

But it clearly wasn't working. The higher the price, the harder and longer the sale. The bigger the projects, the more project management and endless revisions. The longer the timelines, the farther into debt we seemed to sink.

I was juggling too many things, and it felt like I was reinventing every piece of our business every time I did it.

That fateful night in March, while I sobbed into my baked ziti listening to Jewel on repeat, Steve looked across the table and said, "What about those one-day projects?"

He was talking about this little experiment we'd done a year earlier.

I was complaining to my coach that everyone I spoke to who was interested in working with us had no budget for the $30,000 projects I was looking for.

"How much money do they have?" he asked.

"Like $3,000." I laughed at the absurdity. How mismatched we were.

So he challenged me: What *could* you offer for $3,000?

It was so far away from what we were doing, these big

projects over months. But I realized we could actually do quite a bit *if* the clients would get out of our way.

That's when we created a stripped-down offer for the small business owners who loved our work but couldn't afford our new prices. We called it the **Brandup**. They got us for a day, and as much as we could produce on that day, for $2,995. Usually, it was a simple logo, a 1-to 3-page website, and some business cards. But framing it as one day meant no endless revisions. Just us, focused, creating as much as possible in eight hours.

We never promoted it. In fact, we had kept it hidden all year. I'd only bring it up when someone balked at $30,000.

Yet the clients who said yes to the Brandup *loved it.* They came in ready to be decisive and get as much work out of us as they could, which we wanted, too. They always walked away thrilled.

And when I finally did the math, I realized something that changed everything: those little $3,000 days were actually way more profitable than our giant $30,000 projects. This was because our $30,000 projects were spread over months, hours worked every week on both the project and on admin (emails, meetings, follow-ups). All of that added up to about 30 full days of work.

But if we had replaced those 30 days of work with 30 one-day projects at $3,000 each, we would have made $90,000. And $90,000 is obviously much more than $30,000—and therefore, much more profitable.

That night, staring at $40,000 of debt, we finally saw what had been right in front of us the whole time:

The Default Model we were copying was killing us. The scrappy, one-day project we had been embarrassed to show off was the thing that actually worked.

So we made the scariest—and best—decision of our business: we cut all the BS from our business overnight. We let our two high-priced employees go, stopped chasing big, bloated projects, stopped writing fat proposals for free, and went all-in on tight, clear, simple Intensives.

It was the moment everything changed.

Why We All Default to the Default Model

A little girl was helping her mom prepare a pot roast. Right before sliding it into the oven, her mom chopped off the ends.

"Why'd you do that?" the girl asked.

"That's how my mom always did it," she shrugged.

So the girl called her grandma and asked her the same question. Same answer: "That's how my mom did it. That's just the way it's done."

Still unsatisfied, she went to the source—her great-grandma, now in a nursing home.

Great-grandma laughed. "Oh, honey, I just did that because my oven was too small. If I didn't cut the ends off, the roast wouldn't fit."

That's the Default Model in a nutshell. You do it that way because that's just the way it's always been done. You follow what everyone else is doing—hourly billing, retainers, bloated proposals—without ever asking if it actually makes sense. You inherit habits from people who inherited them from someone else, long after the original reason stopped mattering.

And just like cutting the ends off a roast, the Default Model throws perfectly good profit in the trash.

I think I know how this happened.

Most small service businesses enter entrepreneurship like we did—not with an MBA and a clear business plan, but with a skill and a desire for autonomy. You may have looked at the work you were doing inside your previous job at a bigger company, compared what clients were paying to what you were making, and thought, "How hard could it be to find just a couple of these clients myself who can pay me directly? They'll pay less than they're paying now, I'll make more than I was making then, and I'll finally have the freedom I've been craving. Win-win."

Maybe you're like Erika, who left a job as a project manager at a small agency to go out on her own, and ended up pitching and running projects exactly the same way she had at her old job (full of BS).

Or maybe you're like Aaron, who started selling his video work hourly because that's how he got paid as a freelancer, and it felt like the only way to guarantee he'd get paid for his time.

Basically, most people default to one of two modes of operation:

You copy the only business model you've seen (the company you worked at previously). That means free proposals, pitch decks, estimated hours, long timelines, scope creep, and endless revisions.

Or you default to **hourly freelance** because it feels "safe."

At least if you're working, you're getting paid. (Until you realize there's a ceiling, and time off equals zero income.)

Either way, you don't immediately see that the math actually works against you.

You start each month at zero with a number you *must* hit to afford your bills and live to see another day. Feast or famine becomes the norm because you're either hustling with client work or you're hustling to find your next clients when the work dries up. You left your job because you didn't want a boss, but you slowly realize your *clients* have become your boss. If you manage to take a vacation, you end up tethered to your laptop for a chunk of it and find yourself thinking about it when you're not. Your business keeps you busy 24/7, and you feel constantly overworked and underpaid—missing the very freedom you left a job to find in the first place.

Your nervous system gets so used to feeling stressed that *even when things are going well* you're waiting for the next shoe to drop. It's hard to feel good, even in a great month.

In fact, if you're "successful" inside this model? It can get even *worse*!

That's because success means more projects with more moving parts to manage: an inbox filled with important client emails that need a fast response and multiple deadlines to meet each week. You hire help to keep up, and then suddenly you have overhead, payroll, and a new burden: you're still responsible for the client, the quality, and the sales, but struggle to get the hired help to deliver to your standards. You often end up editing—or even redoing—some of the work you paid someone else to do.

Plus, now you must feed the machine, which means *more* sales are needed at a faster clip. You realize you need to raise prices to pay for all this, but then you have to justify those higher prices, so projects and deliverable lists quickly grow to meet and exceed the increased price. The work gets diluted when design-by-committee waters down your brilliant ideas to appeal to the lowest common denominator. By the time a project is finished, you're so tired you don't even care that they got rid of your favorite part. You're just hoping they send the last payment without issue.

And for *all* of these reasons...your time disappears.

And you realize the treadmill you're now on feels *a lot* like the job you left to get off of.

And you wonder: if this is ever going to change? Was making this change even worth it?

Ask me how I know.

Where Most Experts Go Wrong

The problem was that we were working all the time and weren't making enough money. So I assumed the solution was obvious: we needed more clients, with bigger budgets.

But that solution would not have solved the core problem. Closing more clients with bigger budgets would have only added more clutter: more clients, more complexity, more systems to manage, and more people to hire. We would have needed to land even *more* projects just to support the infrastructure needed for the bigger projects. The business would have grown, but the chaos would have grown with it.

The problem wasn't that we were not skilled. And it *wasn't* that we couldn't find enough clients.

The problem was that we had been trying to build what we thought was a "real business" with employees, selling big, premium services, and working with lots of clients. Unfortunately, we hired employees before our offers were profitable enough to reliably cover their salaries, but we didn't know that. Because our process was unprofitable, it only took closing a few clients to go from feeling desperate for work to becoming completely overwhelmed with projects we couldn't handle ourselves.

Thinking that hiring help would solve our problem was a core mistake.

The solution was understanding our business model and pricing our offers profitably, so that if and when we chose to hire, we wouldn't end up paying out all our revenue to the team, to our own financial detriment.

I cannot tell you how many students I have had to coach through this very uncomfortable truth. They're making a lot of money, but they're not keeping much of it because they hired before their projects were actually profitable. It's an easy diagnosis: you have a team, you generate revenue… but you still don't make enough. Or—even without a team—you work constantly on projects and still don't make enough. Both are clear indicators that your offers are unprofitable.

The frustrating part is that I can teach people how to find and close ideal clients and sell $20,000 to $30,000 a month. What I cannot stop them from doing is turning around and paying all of that money to someone else, then wondering why they are still struggling to pay themselves.

Sometimes this hesitation is simply because people already have a team in place. The idea of letting those people go and taking the work back on themselves feels like sliding backward instead of moving forward. It's also emotionally difficult to let go of people you like working with and feel proud to support.

Letting someone go can feel like you failed as a business owner, or failed the people who trusted you with their livelihood. There's a deep pride in building a business that supports not just you, but other people and their families. There is pride in being able to pay people well. I feel this too. We finally get to be the boss, and we want to be a benevolent one.

But none of this actually works if you are not paying yourself enough. It's not impressive to run a business that generates a lot of revenue only to hand it all over to payroll. A business is only profitable and sustainable if you are also being paid fairly and consistently for your work. If that is not happening, then the hard question becomes unavoidable. What is the point of owning the business at all?

I remember many conversations with Emily Wilkins in the early days of working with her, when she was deeply committed to a team that included one close friend. Emily is the owner of Marketing Metal, a branding and design agency that specializes in small manufacturing shops. While she was generating solid revenue, the business wasn't yet profitable enough to support both her team and herself. In practice, that meant she was subsidizing payroll at the expense of paying herself.

When she finally made the decision to let her friend go, a huge weight lifted off her shoulders—and her overhead. That gave her the space to simplify her process, refine her offers, and deliver the work herself while keeping all of the revenue.

What changed was not her ability to sell. She had always been able to close clients. What changed was what she kept. Almost overnight, she went from generating about $15,000 a month and taking home only a few thousand dollars to taking home the full $15,000 per month. At the same time, she went from feeling overwhelmed and like she was constantly "on" to feeling like she had plenty of time to take care of herself and build authority as the go-to expert in her space.

These common business model mistakes remind me of when I used to make a lot of my own clothes in college. My girlfriends and I would go to Joann Fabrics, pull out our sewing machines, and spend the afternoon "stoned crafting." (I went to Wesleyan. What did you expect?)

But I'm not a trained seamstress, and I'm also impatient, which means I made most of my clothes by holding stretchy fabric up to my body, pinching it together where it should be sewn, and then immediately throwing it under the needle to add a stitch. Sometimes it worked alright, and other times it was a total bomb and a waste of material. It would bunch weirdly, or not fit, or just look messy, even though it looked so cool when I draped it.

What I needed was a *pattern*—something that showed me the correct size and shape of the fabric panels I needed to make the garment I wanted.

Instead, for every piece I actually wore, I tossed three that didn't work into the trash.

And that was fine—because it was a hobby, not a business

meant to support my life.

Building your business without a clear model is like trying to make clothing by pinching fabric, throwing in a stitch, and crossing your fingers. Except you can't afford to try out a bunch of businesses in the process, throwing out most of them and hoping one of them sticks.

You need a pattern to follow.

Enter The No BS Business Model

The No BS Business Model is for small, expert-led businesses that want to maximize profit *and* freedom without a big team. It is based on the idea that when your skills are the value the business offers, and you're wearing all the hats to run the business, you simply cannot succeed if your world is overloaded with too many things; the time just isn't there. Your business plan must be so simple that you can carry the whole thing around in your head. Anything more is overcomplicated.

The No BS Model means simplifying your business down to:

1. One Freedom Number
2. One Core Market
3. One Sales Mechanism
4. One Killer Outreach Strategy
5. One Delivery Process

There will always be endless options and too many ideas. But when you simplify and focus your efforts on the five categories above, you can *do fewer things better*. If expertise is about being highly skilled in one thing over many, then becoming an expert in your business naturally requires you to focus on becoming more skilled in fewer lanes.

The clearer this is on paper, the clearer it will be to execute.

Imagine waking up every morning knowing there is just one thing you need to focus on that day. And imagine having confidence that focusing on that one thing is the right move because it's in service of the business you want. Most of us crave that kind of clarity.

But it doesn't just feel good.

If you want freedom and ease, *you need profit.* And if you're selling expertise—where your services are inherently reliant on your time—*the numbers have to work in order to be profitable.* That's just common sense. (Maybe I should have called it the Common Sense Business Model!)

The precious hours you *do* have available to work (while also protecting your freedom time) simply cannot be wasted, either feeling guilty about all the things you think you should be doing, or doing things that aren't actively moving you toward your **one clear Freedom Number**.

So let's start with that.

What is my Freedom Number?

If you ask most expert-based business owners how much money they want to make in a year, there are generally three main buckets of responses:
- "Six figures"
- "$10,000, $20,000, or $30,000 a month"
- "$250,000 or $500,000 a year"

After hearing this from literally thousands of people, it's clear that most haven't done the actual math needed to figure out what they *really* want and need. These are vague ideas that sound good but often aren't taking into account the factors that would actually make the number accurate.

When they say the numbers above, do they mean...

- This is the top-line revenue they want to make *before* any expenses and taxes?
- This is what they want to make after taxes?
- This is what they want to personally take home after business expenses *and* taxes?

Most people don't know which of these it is. If I ask, they'll quickly say, "I guess this is what I personally want to take home." But if you personally want to take home $100,000, and you run your own business, you're going to need to generate quite a bit more than $100,000 in a year.

On top of that, while "I want to make $X/month" *is* a goal, it has little meaning if it's not tied to actual lifestyle choices. And it can be very hard to stay motivated building your business for an abstract amount of money.

So instead, I want you to figure out what your Freedom Number is. It's the revenue you need to generate that will pay for the business and life that you want, including the taxes you will owe.

Here's how to do it. I've created a simple calculator to figure out your Freedom Number scalesolobook.com/resources—but first, I want to explain it briefly so you can get the concept:

Start by adding up all your actual household expenditures

for the year. Include *everything:* obvious items like your rent/mortgage, groceries, car payments, kids' education, but also the bigger expenses each year like vacations, saving for an emergency fund and retirement, and house upgrades. We're going to calculate based on your *needs*: what are all the expenses you currently have that will give you a life of contentment where you are not living an outlandishly lavish lifestyle, but you're also not scrimping.

This should be a life you would feel happy living if you could live it without stressing, without working nights and weekends, and with the freedom and flexibility you crave.

This is the personal income needed.

Now, take that number and divide it by 0.7 (this quick-and-dirty formula assumes a 30% average tax rate and is meant for estimation purposes only). So if your personal income number above was $200,000, then $200,000/.7 would equal approximately $286,000. This is the total personal income you would need to generate in order to pay 30% in taxes and take home the $200,000 you need to afford your life.

Now let's talk business expenses, because you can't run a business for free.

Total up what it costs to run your business right now, including investments you should be making each year to increase its value. This includes SaaS subscriptions, maybe your VA, possibly office space, and definitely marketing (networking events, content support) and skills development (continuing education, consultants and/or coaching).

Take that total—let's say it's $35,000/year because when you're an expert your overhead can be pretty low—and add it to the total income above: $35,000 + $286,000 = $321,000.

All of a sudden, "I want to take home $200,000 personally" means I need to generate $321,000 in revenue.

Quite a different picture! Imagine you're running your business, hustling to get to $200,000, and if you do, you're actually only 60% of the way there.

Even if that number is much higher for you, knowing what it is—and tying it to a tangible set of costs—gives us a basis for developing our offers, prices, and delivery times.

In this scenario, the person's actual Freedom Number is $321,000, not $200,000.

Luckily, this can also go the other way.

Often, people may say they want to make $30,000/month, or $360,000/year. But when they do the math above, they realize their Freedom Number is more like $175,000. It's not that they can't make more, but when they realize they only need to make $175,000 to live a comfortable life that they would be happy with, it relieves a lot of pressure to *always keep making more*.

The point is, rather than pull a nice-sounding number out of the sky, find the tangible number that is rooted in a real life you want to live so you can plan the fastest path to get there. Just like when you are driving to go out for dinner, you're going to get to the restaurant a hell of a lot faster if you have the address.

When I work with business owners, I have them categorize all of their personal and business expenditures in three categories: needs, wants, and desires. This way, we can generate a good, better, and best Freedom Number, which allows us to hit goal one, and then work toward each successive goal as gravy on top, without carrying the stress of *needing* to hit it.

OK, so now that we know our top-line Freedom Number, how do we hit it?

The next step is to use this number with a formula I developed and shared in my first book, *Badass Your Brand*, called the 50/25/25 Rule to Profit and Freedom.

The concept is simple: When you sell your expertise, and you want freedom and flexibility in your life (i.e., not working on nights or weekends, the ability to go on vacation, take days off, and have a life), your numbers need to work as follows:

- You must generate all your revenue in 50% *or fewer* of your working hours.
- You must dedicate *at least* 25% of your time to working on your business so you keep your pipeline full of hot prospects and continually invest in building long-term value.
- The other 25% of your working hours is flexible "freedom" time—yours to use for personal days you want to take off, but also to reinvest into your business when you want to go faster.

Using the formula, we can plug in your top-line freedom goal, do some quick math based on your offers and how long they take to deliver, and find out exactly what you need to charge to support these goals.

For example, let's say a common project currently takes you 80 hours to deliver, and your Freedom Number is $321,000. According to the formula, that project needs to cost $26,750 to support your financial and freedom goals.

Let's do the Math

To keep it simple, we calculate the 50/25/25 formula on 4-week months and 8-hour days. Since that only adds up to 48 weeks a year, and there are 52 weeks in a year, we've built in a secret bonus month of freedom for you. This is both to keep things simple and to account for all the holidays everyone takes off. This means you have 960 hours a year—or an average of 80 hours a month—to work with paying clients to generate your Freedom Number.

As you'll see later in the book, our minds want to focus on the 80 hours *a month,* but it will benefit you to get in the habit of focusing on the annual number instead. For now, if you want help calculating your Freedom Number and your main offer price point, grab it at scalesolobook.com/resources.

Let's go back to the two numbers above: a Freedom Number of $321,000 and the amount you need to charge for that project to support your goals and get you to that Freedom Number, which is $26,750. If you're currently only charging $10,000 for that package, more than doubling your rate may seem daunting.

So let's talk about what needs to happen to move you from *whatever you're charging now* to *whatever you need to charge to hit those goals.*

The Two Levers

Let's keep going with our example above. You did the math, you're charging $10,000 for a project that needs to command $26,750. There are only two levers you can pull to make your project profitable enough to achieve your freedom goal:

Lever #1: Increase the Real—and Perceived—Value of What You Deliver

When clients believe your work is worth more, they'll happily pay more. This lever is about both the *substance* of your expertise and the *psychology* of how it's packaged.

This is how we do it inside the No BS Model:

- **Turn free "trust-building" work into paid engagements** (so prospects pay to be qualified instead of wasting your time).
- **Package and price your offers with authority** so they're seen as premium solutions, not commodities.
- **Position yourself as a trusted advisor** instead of a vendor, so clients come to you for guidance, not just execution.

When you pull this lever, your prices can rise by 20%, 100%, even 200% or more—without adding any extra hours or overhead.

Lever #2: Decrease the Time It Takes to Deliver

The second lever is about streamlining how you deliver so you can earn more in less time. Most experts are stuck in bloated projects that stretch for months, drain their energy, and let clients take over their calendar.

The No BS approach cuts out all the unnecessary stuff that keeps us overworked, overwhelmed, and underpaid, and shows you how to:

- **Cut projects down from months to weeks**—or even days—without losing value (and even adding value!).
- **Install efficient, repeatable systems** across marketing, delivery, and finances so every part of your business is tight and streamlined.
- **Deliver in focused, high-value Intensives** that clients love, and you can price like the premium expert you are.

Pull this lever and your delivery time shrinks by 20%–50%, or more—giving you back hours, sanity, and the ability to serve fewer clients at a higher profit.

Do both, and everything changes.

When you combine higher value with faster delivery, the numbers *really* start to work in your favor. You stop trading hours for dollars and start running a business that can theoretically give you more and more money—and more and more freedom—the longer you do it (provided you invest the other available hours in developing your sustainable business systems).

If you were to cut the number of hours spent on your project by 50%, from 80 hours to 40 hours, and keep the price the same at $10,000, you could deliver two projects in the same timeframe and bring in $20,000 instead of $10,000. That puts you within reach of your $26,750 Freedom Number. Increase the price of those projects by just a few thousand dollars, and you're there!

That's how our own $30,000 projects, which used to drag out for 6–9 months, eventually evolved into **$40,000+ 2-day Intensives.**

We've helped consultants, strategists, and boutique agencies do the same: earning more from fewer clients, cutting the bloat from delivery, and building businesses that are small on purpose, but mighty in profit.

The healthiest, most sustainable expert-led businesses aren't chasing "growth for growth's sake." They're built with clarity and confidence in what they want and how to get there, which is achieved when you know exactly which levers to pull and how.

But after years of teaching this business model, I've learned that one of the hardest steps isn't necessarily implementing it—it's being open to the possibility that it can work at all. This approach often challenges deeply held beliefs about value, effort, loyalty, and what it means to "earn" money in a service business. Resistance is common, but what's rare—and powerful—are the people who feel that resistance and try it anyway.

I remember when I first met Amanda Dahler, owner of Outspoke Design, which focused on designing presentations for large-scale events. Amanda worked with very high-profile clients, who were often demanding of her time and energy.

Amanda was brilliant, highly capable, a hard worker, and was already making good money, but what she could not imagine was a *different* way of delivering. The $30,000 projects she was closing completely consumed her calendar—days, nights, and weekends over the course of weeks—and she assumed that this was the tradeoff for getting paid what seemed like large amounts of money. Like many self-identified hard workers, she equated *effort* and *time* with *value*—just as I used to.

I suggested that Amanda try something different on an upcoming pitch for a potential project by dramatically reducing and reframing her timeline on deliverables. She was nervous and could *not* imagine this landing with her client, whom she'd worked with before and had a good relationship.

When Amanda came back and told me that the client said *yes* immediately, she was genuinely stunned.

She was about to deliver a $30,000 project in roughly *one-eighth* of the time it would normally take her by shortening the timeline and focusing on the project exclusively until it was finished. That *single shift* cracked it open for her. A few months later, she had her first $90,000 month, and her entire relationship to time, value, and pricing changed.

Amanda was willing to try the uncomfortable, and she got to experience something that she previously thought was impossible *actually work*. She was bold, and it paid off.

Those who are unwilling to try may never know. Luckily, sometimes, those who resist end up benefiting because they're *partnered* with someone willing to take that leap first.

Fani Nicheva and her husband Bob von Elgg ran their agency, Strumb Design, the traditional way. It all looked successful, but felt exhausting. Bob, a seasoned designer, relied entirely on referrals. They were constantly busy with work, yet cash flow was still unpredictable, and feeling stressed was the norm.

When Fani introduced the idea of Intensives and upfront payment, Bob was skeptical, especially when she mentioned charging their entire rate up front. As Fani put it, "He doesn't like change. He doesn't like marketing. He doesn't like 'systems.' And he especially doesn't like changing things with loyal clients. If a client is happy, Bob would rather die than touch the process."

But then he watched her run her first Intensive: $17,000 paid up front, the work delivered in three days—and the client was thrilled.

That's when Bob started to come on board. Not because of the money, although that helped, but because he both realized and witnessed something that was more meaningful to him: *This was actually better for the client.*

If you're running your business without a model, you're essentially trying to make a dress without a pattern. You might feel like you're moving along in the right direction with cutting and sewing, but when you put the garment on at the end, you look like Theo in that Cosby Show episode where Denise makes him a ridiculously ill-fitting shirt (pardon the elder Millennial reference).

The levers are about cutting out the BS that's currently making it impossible for you to hit your numbers, including the sales process BS that's leaving money on the table, and the delivery process BS that makes a project take 80 hours when it could probably take 40-60.

Great! But *How* Do You Pull Both Levers?

You now know the basis of the No BS Model. One clear goal number, tied to the tangible, real-world life you want to live, that dictates the prices you must charge if you want to achieve that life and have that freedom.

How do you pull both levers? That's what the rest of this book is all about!

Take Action

- **What are you doing in your business just because "everyone does it that way?"** Name one thing. Then decide if it's actually working for you or just getting you further from your Freedom Number.
- **What did you *actually* make per hour on your last project?** Count everything—the emails, the revisions, the unpaid proposal work. Write it down. Now ask yourself: is this the business you wanted to build?
- **If you could wave a magic wand and eliminate ONE part of how you currently work with clients, what would it be?** You know what it is–the thing that makes you groan every time. The part that drags projects out or drains your energy. That's probably the first piece of BS you need to cut.

If You Only Do One Thing After This Chapter:

The Default Model isn't broken because you're doing it wrong. It's broken because *it was always broken*. You don't need to work harder inside a bad system. You need a better system. Your Freedom Number is the first step to building one.

  Go calculate it: scalesolobook.com/resources

PART 1: THE NO BS BUSINESS MODEL

PART TWO

No BS Marketing

Have you ever spent an hour (or three) creating a post for social media, only to have it get five likes... one of which was from your mom?

Have you ever gone to a networking event, spent hours hovering over the charcuterie board (instead of what you *really* wanted to do, which was curl up with some Netflix and popcorn), and have *nothing* come from it?

Maybe you've taken the major step of running some paid ads—Facebook or otherwise—and all you got were a few spammy comments from private accounts with a truck as the profile pic. (If so, you know what it might feel like to *literally* set your cash on fire.)

When it comes to marketing, it's not just that there are endless things you *could* be doing; it's that *when* you do them, it feels like trying to fill an inflatable pool with nothing but your cupped hands—a lot of effort with unsatisfying results.

And because there truly are so many things you *could* do, there's this ever-present feeling that you're never doing *enough*. That no matter what you're doing, you *should* be doing more.

Marketing done well requires you to show up as your best, most confident, and creative self. Unfortunately, if your brain is weighed down by all these *coulds* and *shoulds*, it leaves very little space for the creative energy that is required, which means your efforts will have a hard time paying off in the long run.

It's a pretty impossible situation when you think about it. That's probably the reason most people suck at it.

Why Marketing Feels So Overwhelming

Believe it or not, people who teach marketing—people who market about marketing—are *great marketers!*

And great marketing usually uses some form of the following framework for its messaging:

Here's [*this thing that you want*] and here's [*how easy it is to get it*], and you can have it without [*all those things you don't want*].

Example: *Close $10,000 coaching clients with just one phone call without having to dance on social media.*

Because *great* marketers are using *great* marketing to sell you on their *great* marketing strategies, we (marketers included) have this stubborn feeling that there is some secret trick to it all—some magic bullet that others know but we don't. If we only knew the secret trick or had that magic bullet, we'd have all the marketing knowledge we'd need to succeed. (And somehow it would also be easy and require little time and effort.)

That belief leads people to chase shiny objects, but never truly commit—trying new things for a short while, not getting great results quickly enough, and then concluding that the strategy didn't work.

So let's get it all out on the table right now: Marketing is *always* going to require consistent, committed action to succeed. And it usually requires you to develop a new skill or two (which also takes perseverance), *no matter what* the strategy is.

That "Close $10,000 coaching clients with just one phone call without having to dance on social media" was the marketing line that got me to buy a program eight years ago. You know what it required? Learning how to do full-on sales calls and persuade people to buy *on the call.* A tough skill to learn for most people, and something few people *want* to learn. But *that* wasn't in the marketing, because if it had been, nobody would have clicked on it.

There are lots of strategies that will give you positive results if you commit to sticking with them—showing up consistently and incrementally improving your skills. (And of course I am proposing that the strategies I'm sharing with you will work better than others.) But *none* of them will work if you can't show up and commit.

Which brings me to the most important issue:

The True "Secret" of Marketing

The true "secret" of marketing isn't the tactic—it's the mindset, expectations, and commitment of the marketer.

Remember The Wizard of Oz? Dorothy had the power to

go home all along—she just had to click her heels. That's how I think about business owners and their marketing. The real power lives inside you, in your willingness to commit and stick with something long enough for it to work.

Learning the strategy is like, 5% of the work. What makes any marketing strategy effective is taking consistent action, incremental tweaking, and most importantly, sticking with it over time.

I remember when my client Deb Mitchell, a brand messaging strategist for interior designers, came to me feeling overwhelmed. Business had slowed because her marketing had fallen to the side while she navigated some personal matters.

As we talked, she mentioned that earlier in the year, she'd been offering brand messaging workshops inside communities that serve interior designers. Every single time she did one, it led to new leads and clients.

So I asked her a simple question: Why not reach back out to those community leaders who already know, like, and trust you, and offer to do that workshop again?

The lightbulb went on. *Of course* she should keep doing it—it already worked! But like so many of us, she'd stopped doing what was working and went searching for the next shiny idea.

I think most people fail to stick with marketing strategies because, deep down, they really don't believe they will actually *work*. They also have unrealistic expectations of what "working" looks like, and on what timeline.

You also have to define what this means for you. You can only know if something succeeded if you have a goal you're trying to hit in the first place. And even then, you have to make sure the goal is realistic based on what your efforts can reasonably deliver. If you choose to build a referral network and your goal is to bring in twelve $30,000 clients a year, but you are only going to talk to five people a month, that's not likely to happen. Does your goal, expectation, and amount of effort you're willing to deliver need a reality check?

Yes, strategy is important, but success with a good strategy relies on you putting focused effort into *making* it work through incremental improvement.

We all have the ability to become expert marketers who bring in ideal clients in a steady stream. But do you have the stamina and the grit to stick with it until you get there?

That is what will determine your success.

Clear the Marketing Mindset Overwhelm

After working with small businesses for 15 years, I've found most owners carry around a ton of BS in their brain that stops them from taking the exact actions needed to succeed. If you've ever gone to post something on social media about your services, only to hesitate because you imagine someone seeing it and thinking 'gawd they are so slimy just trying to sell me something'—instead of thinking about all the people actively looking for your help who would love to know what it's like to hire you—you know what I'm talking about.

Our tendency is to focus on the negative, or potential negatives, instead of the positives.

I know about this unfortunate head trash because I carry a lot of it around, too. Even if there are 20 positive comments, our brain can't stop thinking about the *one* comment that was negative.

When I first tried paid marketing in 2016, advertising the first version of The No BS Business Model to small service businesses, one of the most effective Facebook ads I ever wrote started with this sentence: "Here's how I grew my 2-person business to $500,000 without social media or paid ads." That ad alone was probably responsible for over $100,000 in sales for me, and I kept it running for over a year as it continued to produce results. It resonated, aligned beautifully with my message, and people clicked and purchased.

But I also got snarky comments calling me out, like: "Can't trust a woman whose paid ads claim to teach you how to not use paid ads."

Now to be clear: different business models lend themselves to different marketing strategies.

Those ads were about *teaching* a business model for service businesses that only need a handful of high-paying clients each year. In that context, paid ads are generally not something I recommend.

But selling a digital product—with a lower price and a goal of volume—is a *different* business model that requires a *different* marketing strategy. It has to sell a significant number for it to be worth the upfront effort and financial investment. The strategy I was using to sell a course was different from the marketing strategy I was *teaching* in that course to sell premium services.

And even though I'm confident in my expertise, I *still* think about those comments when I write marketing copy. Those negative comments actually bothered me *more* than just the standard troll comments (like the tin of actual SPAM gif, which you *will* get if you market yourself online). They hurt because they were accusing me of being a hypocrite, as if I was selling something I wasn't doing myself. And even more frustrating was that the medium didn't lend itself to real conversation or interaction. (I certainly *tried* to explain this difference in the comments, but it fell on deaf ears.)

I share this because it's just one example of how much these negative experiences can stay with us, and then influence how we make decisions about putting ourselves and our ideas out there. I don't even know how many messaging ideas I *didn't* test because I was worried they were going to invite negative comments.

I remember a student of mine sharing that a negative interaction she had at a networking event—where an older gentleman insinuated that she didn't really know what she was doing—left her feeling so insecure that she avoided in-person events again for *years*.

Or the many times business owners have told me that they don't want to do email marketing—which is still to this day one of the most effective marketing strategies for small businesses—because they don't want to be "just another spammy email in someone's inbox."

When left to their own devices, our brains tend to focus more on the negative responses we *might* elicit than on the opportunities we might gain. We let the fear of the person who might not like what you're putting out there dictate how and where we show up, instead of focusing on the people who *do* want to hear from you, and who *will* connect with who you are and what you are saying.

If you're sending emails, no matter how good they are, *somebody* will always see them as spam. You can't stop that. People unsubscribe every time I send out an email. You can't give those people your energy.

Instead, here's what you need to retrain your brain to focus on:

You are only sending emails for the people that *want* to receive them.

You are only marketing to *find* the people that get value from you.

Everyone else? They add no value to you or your business, and you want them off your list (literally and figuratively).

Rewire Your Brain for Marketing

Let's do a quick exercise. I want you to close your eyes and imagine your perfect, ideal client. Imagine them sitting in their house or office, struggling with the very problem you solve, wishing that someone exactly like you would appear before them and solve it.

Do you genuinely *believe* that there are people out there who are a perfect fit for you? People who, if you were just sitting across the table from them, would say, "Oh my goodness, you are *exactly* who I've been looking for. I need to hire you!"?

Because I'm here to tell you that they *do* exist. No matter what stage of business you are in right now, no matter your level of skill, there are people out there who need *your* help.

But right now, they are at their kitchen table, and you are at yours. They don't know that you exist, and they don't know where you are or how to find you.

It's your job as a marketer to find them and make sure they know you exist.

That's what marketing is.

And once you find them, they're not just going to *want* to talk to you, they'll be *ecstatic,* because *you* really are the perfect person to solve their problems!

So... *isn't this exciting?!* <Nudge nudge.>

Your whole job is to go find these people who are *super excited* to meet you because they need *you* to solve their problems.

They are who you're looking for.

You're *not* looking for the people who think, "This email is spam and irrelevant to me," or "Why is this person trying to talk to me?" Those people don't have a problem you can help solve, nor are they the kind of people you want to be hanging out with to grow your business. You can't waste energy trying to help someone who doesn't need or want help, or trying to connect with someone who isn't interested in connection.

So don't worry about those people! And definitely don't give those people any of your precious energy. You need that energy to speak to the people who *do* need your help.

To help you clear those people out of your brain, I want you to give "them" a name. That way, every time you think about them, you can tell them to buzz off.

For me, all the trolls and haters are named Chad. So anytime I catch myself worrying about what Chad will say—from "I already knew that," to "This is boring/not helpful/obvious," to just "SPAM!"—I tell Chad to shut it.

This isn't for you, Chad. Buh-bye!

Chad was never going to buy anyway, so no need to think about him.

If you want a marketing plan that actually works long term, remember: your marketing is intended only for those who want and need it. The "anyone else" will get in the mix—you can't help that—but it's up to them to see themselves out.

Not everyone who hears your message will be a perfect fit. Some will be terrible fits. Those people are background noise. There's nothing wrong with them—they may even be people we call friends! But don't let Chad's opinions dictate how you operate. If you let Chad get in your head, it'll make it infinitely harder to find and help people who are *actually* looking for you.

From now on, focus on looking for those who are genuinely excited to talk to you because they need you. They have a problem that you can solve, and *you're gonna be their hero*.

The No BS Marketing Plan

Let's break down how marketing actually works for a small business selling expertise. It's simpler than it looks.

Getting clients always comes down to four steps:

1. **FIND:** You've gotta find the people who are in your target market.
2. **CONNECT:** You've gotta connect with those people (they need to know you exist).
3. **NURTURE:** You've gotta deepen the connection until you're the obvious choice (they need to like and trust you).

4. **OFFER:** Then you gotta make them an offer (*only* if they have a problem you can solve).

Every client you've ever signed—and every client you will ever sign—moves through these four steps. Sometimes it happens in a single conversation, sometimes it takes years. But those four things always happen.

We want a series of things we can do weekly that constantly put *new* people through these four steps: getting us in front of our target market, giving us the opportunity to connect, and then nurturing them into a sale.

But which strategy are we going to focus on, pour a little "blind faith" into, and triple down on until it works for us?

How Experts Find Profitable Clients Today

When a client is referred to you, they move through steps 1–3 immediately. The referrer has already told them about you, made the connection, and handed you a significant amount of trust and credibility just by vouching for you. When someone I like and respect introduces me to a potential hire, that person arrives with trust already established simply because of who sent them. The credibility in the original relationship transfers to the new one. That is why referrals tend to be easier to close—most of the four-step process is already in motion before you even speak.

Referrals also tend to happen when the person has already admitted that they need what you offer, which covers the first half of step 4—they have a problem you are likely able to solve. That alone makes referrals an easy win. If you dislike selling or believe you're "bad at sales," it makes perfect sense if many of the clients you've received from referrals felt pretty easy to close. All you really had to do was the second half of step 4: present the offer.

In the next chapter I'm going to show you how to nail that part of the 4th step, because even when 3.5 of the 4 steps of finding and closing clients are done for you, it still doesn't mean that you are nailing your remaining half step in a way that supports a No BS business full of profit, freedom, and ease. But we'll get to that in a bit.

In this chapter, we're talking about your marketing plan and how to focus on a strategy that will work for you, so you can stop chasing shiny objects and just show up and take focused, intentional action each week to *keep your pipeline full*.

Let's start here: When it comes to selling expertise, referrals have automatically already gone through 3.5 of the 4 steps of closing clients. So why *wouldn't* that be the goal of all your marketing efforts?

It can be. Creating a marketing system that generates referrals has always been the shortest path to building a profitable service business. It takes focused, intentional effort, but so does *any* marketing strategy that will generate profitable results.

I do want to mention the *other* marketing that so many associate with the magic bullet I mentioned above: Online Authority Content. It's important—and I have been teaching it for years because it works—however I'm not going to focus on it here, and I will say a little about why.

Start with Referrals, Not Content

I believe in the power of content that builds online authority. Writing, teaching, speaking, and publishing force you to clarify your thinking, articulate your point of view, and earn trust at scale. Over time, it can become a powerful engine for attracting aligned clients. But here's the part most people don't want to hear: building real authority content takes *years* of sustained effort. It requires that you spend time developing original ideas, pressure-testing them, and learning how to explain them simply and clearly. This is not work you can outsource or shortcut, even with AI. Without that depth, content becomes generic and forgettable, and in today's AI-saturated landscape, forgettable content fails to convert and immediately flags you as someone *not* to trust.

That's why referral marketing has to come first.

My husband Steve had a mentor in plein air painting who told him that every great artist must "throw out their first hundred paintings." I understood that to mean that developing your skills and finding your point of view requires repetition—getting the reps in first before anything truly great can be created. The same is true for anyone who wants to be excellent and become someone who has something truly special and unique to offer.

That's why every successful business owner with online authority that I know—including myself—started by building real relationships before their content ever "worked." Those early years of networking, conversations, and referrals are where you hone your message, build confidence, and create the first hundred "paintings" you have to throw away.

Content doesn't replace that work; it amplifies it. For most experts, authority content should initially serve two purposes: helping referrals trust you faster and sharpening your thinking. If you prioritize content *before* you've built a referral engine, you risk spending years creating into the void—or worse, going broke while waiting for traction.

My goal is to help you build a profitable business *now*. And the fastest, most reliable way to do that is to put relationships first, content second.

So let's develop your referral marketing strategy together so you have a simple, clear plan of action to bring qualified referrals into your pipeline.

What You Need to Build a Referral Machine

Here's what you need to build a valuable referral machine:

1. **Clarity:** A simple, clear message about who you work with, how you help them, and why you are different.
2. **People**: A warm network of people to speak to (and a plan for building it out).
3. **Leverage:** One Killer Outreach strategy (or a 1KO) that can leverage your time to nurture these relationships into clients and referrals.

Clarity

Most people believe their biggest challenge in finding clients is visibility. They think, "If I could just get in front of the right people everything would change." Visibility matters, of course. But the deeper issue is that most people are not prepared to receive clients in the first place. Even if their ideal client were standing right in front of them, that person would have no idea they were a perfect fit, which means no interest, no relevant conversation, and definitely no sale.

Let's take Will and Sue, an extremely successful, wealthy couple with a daughter turning 16. They want to go all out for her birthday party, and money is no object. They are looking for an event planner who will truly listen to their vision, bring creative ideas, and design an unforgettable, one-of-a-kind celebration for their daughter's big day.

Now imagine Cara is an event planner, and Will and Sue are her absolute dream clients. She would love to plan more big, lavish celebrations where budget is not an issue, and the clients want her to get creative and make something truly special.

Cara meets Will and Sue at an event and strikes up a conversation. She mentions that she plans events. Their eyes light up and they ask what kind of events she does. Cara answers, "I've planned all kinds of events—corporate events, dinner parties, kids' birthdays, weddings. I pride myself on being able to plan an event on any budget." She says this because she wants them to know they should consider her, no matter what they are looking for.

But as premium clients, this does not spark curiosity for them. Cara sounds like every other event planner they have met. Nothing wrong with that, but not what they want. They don't mention their daughter's birthday, but they tell her they will keep her in mind. In fact, the next time their company needs a small luncheon planned, they reach out to her. The budget is low, but Cara is happy to take the work.

Later that evening, they meet Jill. When they ask Jill what

she does, she says, "I plan celebrations people still talk about years later—weddings, milestone birthdays, anniversaries. The kind of events where every detail matters because they only happen once, and cookie-cutter won't cut it. I'm not the cheapest option, but once someone works with me, they come back for every milestone event after."

Jill's confidence, clarity, and focus on high-end celebration design are *exactly* what Will and Sue are looking for, and they practically hire her on the spot. Jill speaks directly to their desire to create a once-in-a-lifetime memory for their daughter.

Cara, who dreams of high-end clients and high-end budgets, will continue to believe she is not getting in front of the right people. What she does not realize is that she *is* meeting the right people. They simply do not see her as the best option, all because of how she is positioning herself.

Bottom line: You can only attract the kinds of clients you are positioned and prepared to receive.

How To Find Your Clarity

When you run a tiny shop, you don't have the luxury of wandering. You're the CEO, the marketer, the salesperson, the service provider, and sometimes the entire backstage crew. You can't afford to waste time reinventing the wheel with every new client. And you certainly can't afford to build a business where the only way to make more money is to work more (you're probably working more than enough as it is).

One of the core principles of a No BS Business is simple: Charge more while working less and getting your clients *better* results.

But that only works if your process is streamlined, repeatable, and constantly improving. You can't master a process you only use once in a while. You become an expert by running the same play over and over—refining, tightening, and elevating it every time.

That's why choosing a niche is non-negotiable, and it's not as limiting as you likely think.

Why "Industry Only" Niching Is a Trap

Most people hear "niche" and think "industry." That's one way to niche, but it's not the only way. Sometimes choosing *only* an industry can create more complexity, not less. If you say you build websites for IT companies, your network might think you're a good fit for:

- A solo IT consultant with a simple, five-page site.
- A 100-person IT firm with 20 stakeholders, and a 50-page site.

Those are not the same project, not even close. The goals, process, and deliverables are different, and the number of opinions involved is wildly different. If you're size-agnostic, you're process-agnostic—and that's where your time and profit disappear.

An effective niche isn't always an industry. It can be a stage, a role, a revenue level, a business model, or a very specific problem (or the intersection of several of those) anchored by a process *you* develop and run better than anyone else.

Why Process Fit Matters More Than Industry

To deliver higher and higher value in less and less time, you need clients who fit into a process you can execute in your sleep. That's why we don't necessarily need to niche down by industry as much as we do by *client type* and *company size*.

For us, that's 1- to 3-person service businesses that want to charge premium prices. Someone who wants to be the cheapest option on the market is not my person. And even though my niche includes many industries, it works—because within that slice of the market, my process delivers beautifully every single time, no matter the industry.

The businesses in our niche all have the same fundamental business model, similar inputs (time and expertise), and similar goals (make more money in less time). Which also means they have the same general brand, copy, and website needs. And after working with hundreds of them, I can tell you they have the same predictable questions, variations, and decision-making challenges.

That means our work can be custom, but the *process* is not.

That's how you deliver better results with less effort. That's how you become known as an expert. That's how you scale your profit and freedom.

How to Pick Your Niche (The No BS Way)

Forget picking a niche out of thin air because it sounds fun or trendy. The best way to choose a niche is by looking at the clients you've already worked with—preferably ones who've already paid you. Here's a quick way to do it:

1. **List the clients who have paid you the most** in the last couple of years. (If they paid, the market exists.)
2. **List the clients you enjoyed working with the most.** (If you enjoyed them, you can enjoy more of them.)
3. **List the clients or projects that allowed you to do your best work.** (If you did your best work, that's where your value is highest.)

When you compare those three lists, you'll usually see a pattern of the kinds of clients who appear more than once. That's your first big clue.

If you end up with multiple strong niches, great. Now you have options. At that point, you're not choosing between a "good niche" and a "bad niche"—you're choosing between good and great. Choose one, or keep working with both until one emerges. Or choose based on who you are more connected to.

You're looking for past clients who:

- You delivered real value for
- Valued your expertise
- Could afford to pay premium prices (or had the ability to)
- Ideally resemble other past clients (which means there are more of them out there!)

Because where there is one, there are hundreds. We only pick a niche once we have real-world data to support that choice, because then we know the niche has been validated.

If you don't have a clear idea of who you are best suited to help and how you uniquely help them, I want to give you the first practical, actionable piece of advice that will help you figure it out right now: Put yourself out there, and talk to and work with lots of clients.

If you haven't been doing this, and have been getting clients primarily from referrals that come to you, then you haven't been learning what resonates about you in the real world. It took hundreds (thousands!) of conversations for me to go from "We are graphic designers for small businesses" to "We build Badass Brands without the BS for 1-3-person service businesses in 1-3-day Intensives." The latter got people interested in hearing more. It was memorable, and got me clients and referrals. The former got me a lot of crickets.

You need to be talking to new people—consistently—to learn what actually resonates. The only way to understand what clients value most, what you love delivering, and what's most profitable is by working with real clients, over and over again. Until then, any claim about your differentiator is just a hypothesis. The fastest path to clear positioning is getting your reps in: serving clients, building a referral engine, and testing what sticks in the real world. Once you have that data, a brand strategist can help you distill it into a clear, compelling positioning grounded in lived experience—not theory.

It's very hard for anyone, including brand strategists, to do this for themselves because we know too much. We are attached to many of our ideas, and we're often too close to our own work to simplify and cull them into something simple and clear.

It takes guts to own a simple message and a specific audience—especially when you *can* help all kinds of people in many different ways. What if being specific means leaving money on the table? That's the fear. We saw it with Cara. She only wants to do high-end events—she's already done a few—but she's scared that owning that positioning will scare off potential clients. So she stays broad, trying to be everything to everyone. But what she'll never know is how many *dream* clients passed her by because her message wasn't clear. She's trying to avoid losing money by staying broad, but ends up losing the very people she wants to attract.

Now, Cara may not be quite ready to own the high-end event space yet. Maybe she's only done a couple of these types of events, and she needs cash to keep coming in each month. She's not in the position to double down on that market just yet.

This is what the reps are for.

Jill put in the reps. She started out just like Cara. And over time, as she booked more and more jobs, she did everything she could to do bigger and bigger events. She went above and beyond what she was paid to do for her larger event clients because she wanted to specialize in that kind of work. Jill made those events extra special and unique, and it paid off. She delighted those clients so much that they were more than willing to keep bringing her back. And when she asked for introductions to their friends who might be hosting events soon, they were happy to make those connections.

Once Jill had a solid portfolio of the kinds of clients she *really* wanted, that's when she went all in on her brand and message. And that took guts. She knew she was going to scare away the smaller clients who still paid the bills. But she also knew that owning the big clients was the only way to become known in that space.

Once you've put in the reps, you'll have enough intel to know your niche, and you'll be ready to hone your message into a clear and memorable statement.

If you pick a group to target before you've actually worked with enough of them to know they're the right fit, you might struggle to attract or close them and have no idea why. Sometimes it's just that this type of client doesn't hire solo operators until you've built real authority and credibility in their world—and that takes time. You simply need to work your way up to those types of clients.

I see this all the time: someone leaves a job at a bigger company or agency where they worked with large clients. They strike out on their own and try to target the same types of clients. After all, they've led big projects, they know the landscape, they've got the experience. So why wouldn't those companies hire them now?

Well, because they didn't hire the person as a solo consultant, they hired a company with a reputation. This person happened to run the project, backed by the *company's* credibility. On their own, that individual does not have the foundation yet to get that client. And unless they have an existing "in" through their relationships, they will struggle to find and close those larger companies as clients. So the path to niching with large companies is either to use existing relationships to get a few clients under your belt (since you already have credibility through those relationships) or to work with smaller clients and work your way up.

Benjie Hughes, the owner of *Hopeless Marketing*, is a great example of how experience alone isn't the same as market credibility. For more than 20 years, he led major projects for large companies while working at an established agency. When he left to start his own consultancy, he assumed those same large clients would naturally follow. But he quickly ran into a familiar wall: those companies hadn't hired *him* before; they had hired the firm behind him. Without that institutional reputation or any direct relationship leverage, closing big clients as a solo operator was far harder than it looked on paper.

The shift came when Benjie, instead of aiming exclusively at larger companies, started focusing on three "thresholds" that signal a client needs his help: big growth goals, planning an exit, or preparing for a pivot or merger. After attending a local manufacturing summit, he followed up thoughtfully with people who caught his attention—some in his ideal audience, some not. One of those outliers turned into a $25,000 client: a small SEO agency with strong technical expertise but unclear messaging. They weren't his original ideal client, but they met two of his three fit indicators, and by clearly communicating his process, Benjie built trust quickly. The deal didn't come from chasing the biggest names in the room; it came from expanding his definition of fit (for now) while he works up to the larger businesses he is accustomed to.

It all comes down to this: the clarity of your message directly affects the effectiveness of your marketing. And you find that clarity by taking action and getting in the reps of sharing your message and working with clients.

Your Turn: Write Your Clarity Statement

There are entire books dedicated to finding your category-of-one positioning, because the better your message is, the better the results of your efforts will be. But even just a simple sentence that clearly states who you work with and how you help them—and ideally why you do it differently—will go a long way.

If you don't have a clear niche yet, you can still add specificity. For example, instead of saying you work with "small businesses," clarify the size and type of company you typically serve. A company with 10-50 employees is very different from a six-figure solopreneur. You might also notice that your clients tend to come to you at a particular turning point in their business, and that moment is what prompts them to seek help. When you include details like these, the person hearing your description can immediately picture specific people they know, and that makes you far more referable.

For example, my friend Liz coached female small business owners. We had known each other for *years,* and although I knew many small business owners, she never really came to mind as someone I should refer them to. Then one day, she said something that really stuck with me. One of her clients was bringing in around $500,000 a year and needed her help transitioning into a million-dollar business with a solid team. The transition from a solopreneur with a few contractors to a business with full-time employees was *exactly* what she helped so many of her clients with.

A few weeks later, I was having brunch with my friend Dana

who pretty much said word for word, "I'm doing really well on my own right now, but I'm looking toward the next phase of my business with an in-house team, and I'm ready to build a million-dollar business."

Immediately I thought of Liz, made the intro, and Dana hired Liz on the spot. Because of the clarity and specificity in her message, Liz came immediately to mind when Dana described her situation. Had I not heard Liz describe her niche with that level of specificity, I would never have thought of her at that moment.

This demonstrates the power of having a clear message. Without one, you simply aren't coming to mind. Having a specific and memorable message is like buying a piece of real estate in people's minds—they'll think of you immediately when they encounter your ideal client.

The best way to get specific is to look at what you've already done. Make a list of the kinds of clients you've worked with and pick out 3-5 that you would like more of. Even if you *could* work with everyone, it's going to be much clearer if you say "I work with small businesses—some of my recent clients include lawyers, architects, and interior designers—and help them manage their cash flow as their outsourced CFO," than if you just say, "I work with small businesses as their outsourced CFO." Just by mentioning a few examples, the listener forms a picture of the kind of person you work with, and people they know that fit that description come to mind. The person you're talking to begins to connect the dots, and refer you.

People

Building a referral machine relies on having a network of people that know, like, and trust you.

Now, you might already have a decent network. Perhaps you've been in business for a while, and/or you naturally connect with people and stay in touch. If that's the case, these strategies are going to supercharge your business—and reliably attract ideal clients to you—by stoking the fire in a systematic way.

If you don't have a network, and you've never put effort into building one or getting your name out there, there are some things you will need to do to get started.

Either way, the first step is to make a list of who you know. Do some digging and make the longest list you can. We always start with who you know because the fastest way to build a network *starts* with the network you already have. Why would we start from scratch when we could start on third base?

Make a list of everyone who knows you: past clients and colleagues, friends and family, old connections from organizations you were a part of and schools you went to, people you are connected to online, and anyone you have met while running your business.

You'll realize you know a lot more people than you think.

That doesn't mean everyone's a winner. As soon as you read that list, I bet you thought, "Just because I went to school with them doesn't mean they are in my network. I haven't spoken to them in 20 years!" Or, "I haven't spoken to the people I worked with at that job in a decade. I don't really know them anymore."

You're not wrong. Some of these people may be a dead end. But you'll never know *which* people are a dead end until you make the list and reach out to them.

The goal is to reconnect with everyone in your network and establish a foundation. From there, we need a simple system to continually nurture and develop those referral relationships.

The next step after you've made your list is to give everyone a simple score of 1-5 in two categories: how likely they are to be connected to an ideal client, and how much they know, like, and trust you. 5 is the highest score in both categories.

For example, if "Jane" is a friend and colleague, and happens to be connected to lots of business owners—and my clientele is business owners—then I would give her a 5 in each category.

If "Drew" is my oldest childhood friend, and has been an elementary school teacher his entire career, I might give him a 5 in know/like/trust, but a 1 in likelihood to be connected to my ideal client.

I created a resource to keep your list organized and all in one place, so you can analyze everything together. It will prompt you to first make a list of your contacts, then go through and rate them. Find it at scalesolobook.com/resources.

Once you rate everyone, you'll sort them by their total score, with the highest scores being your best connection opportunities, and the lowest scores being your least likely opportunities.

This helps you get honest about what your network looks like. Anyone with a score of 8 and above is a strong connection for your business. These are your **tier one connections**.

Those who scored a 5-7 are opportunities to explore. They're your **tier two connections**.

Scores of 4 and below are the least likely to benefit you, but are there to be evaluated on a case-by-case basis. They are your **tier three connections**.

Your goal at first is to shake the tree. This means connecting with your top two tiers (one conversation at a time) to start finding new clients immediately.

During this phase you will also be evaluating who is worth building deeper relationships with, and who isn't.

Once you figure out who your core network really consists of—the people you actually enjoy connecting with and want to invest in, versus those who aren't worth the effort—you can start developing your network into something that works for you. From there, we create a strategy for maintaining and strengthening those relationships over time.

Building Your Network

When I first started my business in 2011, I was 27 and convinced I had no network. In reality, I knew plenty of people from high school, college, and the random gig jobs I'd worked in my twenties—it just never occurred to me to reach out to them.

I first learned the word "networking" when a client I found on Craigslist invited me to visit her BNI (Business Network International) networking group. At the time, Craigslist was my entire client acquisition strategy, so when I discovered BNI, I thought I had found the secret path to getting clients.

Like I do with most things, I went all in. I joined a chapter, booked one-on-one coffee dates with every other member, got introductions to their contacts, explored other networking groups, and started showing up to evening events. New York City is full of opportunities to meet people in person, so once I tapped into that world, momentum built fast. Everyone I met was also growing their network, so simply sharing what I did and who I wanted to meet caused my connections to multiply quickly. Before long, my days were stacked with back-to-back coffees, morning meetings, and evening events.

It was *grueling*.

Within a few months, I began running into the same people in different rooms. And as introductions kept happening, people kept asking if I knew a woman named *Jean Tang*. When I said I didn't, they all seemed surprised. She was a copywriter, I was in branding and design, and everyone else had already decided we were a perfect fit. Her name kept coming up again and again.

The anticipation built—who was this *Jean Tang* lady and why did everyone know her?

And that's when it clicked for me: *I wanted to be like Jean Tang*. I wanted to be the person that everyone mentioned to others and said, "How do you not know Pia Silva? You must meet her!"

So I doubled down on showing up to everything and meeting everyone. Six months later, I sat down for coffee with someone who said, "Pia, literally everyone I talk to mentions your name and says I have to meet you!"

Success! I had reached Jean Tang status!

Oh, and I finally *did* connect with Jean, and everyone was

right: we clicked instantly and became fast friends who stood the test of time. She has remained one of my closest friends and business confidants for nearly 15 years.

I'll admit that those first couple of gruelling years of networking often felt like a waste of time. I had to *kiss a lot of frogs*, so to speak, to make the handful of connections that actually turned into clients. There were plenty of hour-long coffees with "insurance salesman" types that went nowhere and were sometimes painfully dull.

At the time, every client I had came from those conversations—some great, some… not so much. But the real value was this: those were the years when I was finding my voice, shaping our brand, figuring out how to run a business, and learning how to position our offer in a way that resonated. I didn't realize it then, but every conversation was doing that work for me. I was building my communication skills and my network at the same time. The work paid the bills, but in retrospect, the payoff was much bigger.

I was learning who we were, and what made our work valuable.

Of course, at the time it didn't feel like it was paying off much. We were stuck in the feast-or-famine cycle, hustling from project to project. Then, in 2014—at our lowest financial point—we switched to the No BS Model, and everything clicked. We finally found clarity, shifting from "we do graphic design, branding, and websites for small businesses" to "we build badass brands without the BS in 1–3 day Intensives for 1–3 person service providers."

Not only had the hundreds of conversations I'd had over

the years helped me hone my message and gain experience across many types of projects, but all of the people I'd met and nurtured suddenly became a far more powerful referral network than I ever could have imagined. I had built the network while finding my way—and when I finally landed on brand and messaging that worked, the network was already there.

I went back to everyone I knew, shared our new positioning and offer, and suddenly the people who already knew, liked, and trusted us began referring ideal clients with ease. What once felt like chasing clients on an endless treadmill turned into a steady flow of the right work coming our way.

How to Build and Nurture Your Network

The first step is to build your network by connecting with **more people who are connected to your ideal clients**. You can do this in two ways:

- Meeting new people through **your existing connections**
- Meeting new people through **live events**

I did both. I was constantly meeting new people at events and intentionally following up with the people I clicked with. I asked everyone I met for introductions, clearly explaining who I work with, the kinds of referral partners I wanted to meet, and who would benefit most from being connected to me.

I showed up to events a few times a week for more than a year, until I had built enough warm relationships to stop chasing new rooms and start doubling down on the network I already had.

And yes—meeting people in the real world takes time. That's exactly why I am going to teach you the One Killer Outreach strategy(1KO). It helps you leverage that time, deepen relationships faster, and expand your network without burning yourself out.

Leverage

Once I had built a sizable warm network of colleagues and fellow business owners, I became more discerning about who I met with. I shifted from quantity to quality, focusing on deepening existing relationships and meeting people who came through trusted introductions.

This is why I started hosting gatherings. They gave me:
1. A personal reason to reach out to people I wanted to stay in touch with
2. A way to give value without asking anything in return
3. Time in person with multiple tier-one and tier-two connections at once
4. The chance to be seen as a leader and host (which boosted both confidence and credibility)
5. An easy excuse to stay connected with new people by inviting them to the next event (which made deepening relationships with new great contacts so much easier)

I hosted three different types of gatherings, each appealing to a different group:
1. **Monthly Marketing Breakfasts** at our studio, inviting only people in branding and marketing—designers,

strategists, web developers, copywriters, and videographers. We all knew we were natural referral partners.
2. **Monthly happy hours** across industries, where I picked a bar and invited people I thought would benefit from meeting one another.
3. **Monthly poker nights** at our studio. Steve and I would staple green felt to three long tables and host a tournament for about 24 people. This only appealed to a specific crowd, but it was the most fun—and by far the most effective—for building real relationships. There is nothing like just hanging out with someone around a poker table for 5 hours to really feel like you are best buds at the end!

I know this can sound like a lot, but once I'd done each type of gathering a few times, the process became simple and repeatable. The key was scheduling dates months in advance so I wasn't constantly planning and always had the next event ready. That meant every time I met someone new, I could immediately invite them to the right gathering. Even when people couldn't attend, they often said they'd love to come to the next one—which gave me a natural reason to follow up and stay connected. Some never made it to an event at all, but the consistent invitations kept the relationship warm. Over time, I became someone people saw as highly active, well connected, and someone they wanted to stay close to.

If hosting sounds intimidating, you're in good company. Most people immediately jump to the worst-case scenarios: what if no one shows up, or the whole thing feels awkward? Often, though, the real discomfort is just being visibly in charge as the host.

Sarah Salvatoriello, the strategic force behind *Ampersand & Ampersand,* a brand strategy and design studio for founder- and female-led businesses, felt that fear too. She's an introvert, and when she first came up with the idea of hosting a "Ladies Wine & Design JC," she only felt comfortable doing it with a friend. Having a co-host felt safer, like there was someone else to share the weight and the responsibility if the room was quiet or the turnout was small.

But each event made the next one feel a little easier. When her co-host eventually moved to California, Sarah decided to keep going on her own. Her confidence continued to grow with each event and now, the monthly salons regularly sell out, often with a waitlist! What once felt scary has become something she genuinely enjoys.

While hosting events is powerful, it's not required. If you don't have a space or aren't ready to plan something yourself, attending events is a great place to start. Even when I was just a guest, I practiced *acting* like the host. Walking into a room full of strangers can feel intimidating—especially when it seems like everyone else already knows each other. Once I realized most people felt exactly the same way, it became much easier to start conversations. I stopped seeing it as awkward and started seeing it as helpful!

For example, whenever I began talking to someone, I'd look for others standing alone and wave them in, introducing everyone to each other. Simply being willing to initiate conversations and make connections often led people to assume I was hosting the event.

Obviously when it *is* your event, it's even more impactful. Hosting naturally positions you as someone people remember, trust, and want to stay connected to—which is exactly what builds a referral-driven business.

But this is where the 1KO really shines: anytime I met someone I wanted to deepen a relationship with, I always had an invitation *ready*—to a dinner, happy hour, or poker night with people already in my orbit. Having an immediate, meaningful next connection makes staying in touch effortless and accelerates relationships without adding more work.

Your Turn: Design Your 1KO

The goal of your 1KO is simple: one clear, focused strategy for leveraging your time to stay genuinely connected to your network. It's about building an inner circle of relationships and helping the people in it grow, so everyone benefits together. Rather than scattering your energy across dozens of marketing ideas, you're choosing one approach you can repeat consistently, without reinventing the wheel every month. That focus makes it far easier to stay top of mind, deepen relationships, and use your marketing time efficiently.

My examples are mostly in person because online group events weren't common when I was building my agency. And it's true that relationships often deepen faster face-to-face. That said, this approach works just as well online now. To this day, I still participate in both virtual and in-person gatherings as a deliberate way to invest in my relationships.

Let's start with the logistics and figure out what will work best for you.

In Person

If you're in a location where building a local network is realistic and worthwhile, I recommend starting with in-person gatherings. The key is choosing an event format that feels aligned with your personality and energy, such as:

- Lunch
- Dinner
- Happy hour
- Something more creative

The first time Eleanor Hancock, the savvy (and self-proclaimed "covert introvert") founder of *Number 75 Design*, hosted a small business gathering in Lincoln, UK, she wasn't trying to build a marketing engine. She was solving a much simpler problem: the loneliness of being a small business owner without coworkers. She started with a small, casual weekly Zoom hangout for local business owners where they could connect and talk about business, visibility, and the reality of doing it alone.

But over time, the weekly Zooms started to feel like a second job. With three kids, a business, and a full life, Eleanor knew that kind of weekly commitment wasn't sustainable. So she closed the Zooms and decided to host one final in-person gathering.

That one night changed everything. She organized a simple meetup at a client's local pizza restaurant. Nothing fancy and no agenda, just fun and social. But people showed up, and they brought friends. People posted photos and almost immediately, those who missed it asked, "When's the next one?"

That's how *Lincs Small Biz* was born. It became a rotating series of in-person events that were fun, varied, and about connecting: axe throwing, gin-tasting, brunch clubs after the school run, a summer dog walk with ice cream, and a sold-out Christmas party. Eleanor hosted exclusively at local independent businesses, often past clients, which quietly strengthened relationships and positioned her at the center of the local business community. Over time, venues began *asking* her to host.

The events became a powerful client-nurturing engine. One attendee booked after overhearing two past clients discussing how they cried in their Lead Product session with Eleanor. Others began following her because their friends tagged them in event photos. Some attend for years *before* becoming clients.

The impact was undeniable. Roughly three-quarters of Eleanor's recent clients came directly from these events or from being aware of the community and seeing her as a leader. Some people attended for *years* before hiring her—but when they were ready, she was the only option for them.

This is a 1KO in action: one repeatable effort that builds connection, authority, and referrals, without feeling like marketing at all.

Tips For Designing Your In Person 1KO

Do something that feels easy to execute and genuinely fun. The lowest-lift, highest-impact option is a meal. Pick a date, time, and location, invite five to ten people, and you're done.

That size is small enough to create real connection without turning it into work.

Here's how I usually run a small dinner.

First, I keep the logistics simple. I let the restaurant know ahead of time that everyone will be on separate checks so there's nothing awkward at the end. When people arrive, I greet them and immediately introduce them to whoever's already there with a little anecdote about them and how we know each other. That sets the tone and immediately sparks conversation.

Once the full group has arrived, I take a minute to explain why I brought everyone together—just a quick intention setting, like wanting to deepen relationships and help each other grow.

Then I run a short round of introductions. I go first to model it and I use a timer because people *will* ramble if you let them. I ask everyone to share their name, what they do, and who they help, plus one fun prompt—a fun fact about them that only their friends/family know, something they're excited about, a favorite book or podcast, an ask they have right now, or one thing they'd love to fix in their business if they could wave a magic wand. The goal is to give people a few extra details to fuel real conversations afterward.

After that, I get out of the way. I let people talk while we wait for food and connect naturally. About halfway through the meal, I'll usually have everyone switch seats—either right when the food arrives or after we eat, before dessert or coffee. This doubles the value if everyone ends up having real conversations with two different sets of people.

By the end of the meal, people have made meaningful

connections, you've spent quality time with everyone, and the entire experience was fun and valuable. Just by hosting it this way, you're positioned as someone who brings people together thoughtfully—and that's what makes you memorable, trusted, and easy to refer.

At the end of the meal, I encourage people to take a moment to reflect on who they met and how they might support each other. I suggest they jot down a few concrete follow-ups—introductions to make, resources to share, or conversations to continue—while it's still fresh. I'll send a follow-up email right then with everyone's contact info so no one leaves wondering how to stay in touch.

Simply organizing a gathering like this positions you as a connector and a resource. You're facilitating meaningful relationships, and that makes you memorable, keeps you top of mind, and makes you far more referable. People refer business to people who clearly have their shit together, and this is an easy way to demonstrate that at scale.

Some of the smartest marketers I know build their businesses almost entirely through relationships. One of the best I've ever seen at this is my friend Selena Soo, author of the fantastic book *Rich Relationships*. I met Selena in 2017 when she invited me to a dinner she was hosting, even though we had never met before. Today, we are in each other's worlds, supporting each other's businesses and book launches. That is the long-term leverage of a single, well-designed connection.

It wasn't just a meal; it was a memorable experience. Selena and her friend Chris rented a private wine cellar at Wine:30 in Manhattan and hosted about 20 of us for dinner, drinks, and intentional connection. They sent an email ahead of time with the guest list, a short blurb about each person, and links to everyone's LinkedIn profiles. By the time we sat down, the room already felt warm, familiar, and full with possibility.

Selena hosts dinners like this regularly, and it is a major reason she has built such a deep, meaningful network. That network did not just feel good. It supported her in building a multi-million dollar business.

But you don't have to pay for the event for it to be impactful. It's the thought and care that go into the guest list and your follow-through that are the real value you are offering your guests.

Online

If you're in a more remote location—or simply don't love in-person events—an online 1KO may make more sense. It gives you access to people anywhere and can be just as effective when it's well designed.

Design your event around a common goal of the people you are inviting. Ask yourself: what is the purpose, and what will be most valuable for them? If you are inviting potential clients, that might mean introducing them to people who can support their businesses or offering education that will help them grow. You could give a short presentation, run a workshop, or host a panel featuring experts your ideal clients can learn from.

For example, Réland Logan, owner of *Gray Digital Marketing*, has a virtual 1KO experience she calls the *Champagne Connection*. Every attendee is a past guest from her podcast, which means there's already shared context, credibility, and trust before anyone ever joins the room. In fact, she started her podcast to give herself a reason to reach out to her ideal clients and connect with them in the first place, then began hosting these virtual events to deepen those relationships.

Each quarter, Réland invites past guests to join and asks them to fill out a short form beforehand detailing what they have to offer the community and what they're hoping to receive. From those responses, she creates a curated deck shared only with attendees, featuring each person's photo, podcast episode, LinkedIn profile, and exactly how they can help or collaborate. Before the event even starts, everyone knows who's in the room and why they're there. During the live session, Réland runs structured, goal-based speed networking and actively facilitates introductions based on who people most want to meet. If certain connections don't happen live, she personally follows up afterward to make sure they do.

The result is a high-trust, no-awkwardness environment that feels collaborative rather than transactional. The *Champagne Connection* generates the majority of Réland's leads and keeps her booked months in advance—often through introductions made by participants. As demand grows, she's now expanding the concept into book talks and in-person gatherings. This 1KO maintains authentic proximity to her ideal clients and referral sources and is a powerful way to keep her pipeline full.

You may also choose to focus your event on bringing together people who serve similar clients to strengthen your referral engine. This was my marketing breakfast—none of my guests were potential clients, but all of *their* clients were.

No matter the format, a great online event requires you to

step fully into the role of leader. People will keep coming back if it's well run and not just another wandering Zoom call. That value comes from clear structure: a strong opening, intentional introductions, a focused topic, and guided breakout rooms. Rotate the groups, bring everyone back together, prompt the conversation, and keep things moving. When you lead confidently and help people connect quickly and meaningfully, the event feels worth their time—and they remember who made it happen.

Hosting these events is also an excellent way to strengthen your presentation and leadership skills and to establish yourself as a leader. If this sounds intimidating, that is usually a sign you are stretching and growing. I've coached many people through their first events, and while they are often nervous at the start, they quickly gain confidence. After a few sessions, they look forward to hosting and are encouraged by the steady stream of thank-yous from people who got real value from being there.

When Lynn Hawthorn, founder of *Physis Publishing* and *Quietly Iconic Brands*, first considered launching a virtual 1KO, she was nervous in two completely opposite ways at once. Part of her worried no one would show up, and another part worried too *many* people would. As an introvert, the idea of hosting something live, being visible, and leading a room felt like a stretch on every level.

She sat with the idea for months before finally deciding to move forward, supported by the No BS community and a conscious choice to be brave rather than comfortable. She launched *The Difference-Makers Monthly Meetup,* an hour-long session where attendees learn something new and connect with one another. She announced it, shared it with her list and contacts, and trusted the process.

These days her 1KO consistently draws between four and seven attendees each month, all seasoned service providers and business owners. Even the smallest group she's hosted, three people, felt intimate and valuable rather than disappointing. Over time, Lynn realized that the key wasn't trying to make it a huge event or forcing herself to perform, it was simply being herself with a clear role as facilitator. Having that structure made hosting feel energizing rather than draining.

Today, Lynn genuinely looks forward to hosting her 1KO. What once felt scary now feels natural and fun. The meetup has become a steady visibility engine, with about half the attendees being past clients and half new connections. People reach out to join, referrals turn into ideal projects, and trust builds naturally. What once felt intimidating is now one of her favorite parts of her business—a reminder that a successful virtual 1KO doesn't need you to be loud or extroverted. You just need intention and the willingness to step into leadership.

Where Authority Content Fits

When I was getting ready to publish my first book, I remember thinking that one of its main purposes was to help people believe in me, and listen to me, so I could better help them. *I* already knew I could help people with their brand and business, but I needed *them* to believe that too—ideally, without having to speak with me first. I knew how I felt about authors whose books had shifted my thinking. If the book was good enough, they could go from complete unknowns to legitimate experts in their field. That was the power of a book, and I wanted it!

This was when I realized I was actually going to have to *put myself out there* if I wanted people to read the book. That was the whole point, after all. *Yikes!* So even though I hated having my photo taken, I knew I needed to hire a photographer and do a real, professional photoshoot. I also had to accept that I'd have to start showing up on social media if I wanted the book to be seen.

That's why Steve and I decided to put my face on the cover—despite warnings from people with far more publishing experience. If this book was meant to establish me as an authority, then seeing my face often would only help.

Around that time, after blogging two times a month for three years, I got the opportunity to write for *Forbes*. It was one of those moments where preparation met opportunity. The friend who introduced me (Jean Tang!) had been writing for them for over a year, as had several other friends. When her editor said they were looking for someone to write about small business branding, she immediately sent them my way—because she'd been reading my emails for three years. I was an obvious choice! And despite my imposter syndrome, I was ready.

These were *really* intentional (albeit uncomfortable!) decisions I made back in late 2016 to go from hiding from the camera and rejecting social media, to going full force in the other direction. It was scary, but I had a clear purpose. I wanted everyone to read my book, and I knew they were far more likely to do that if they felt connected to the real person who wrote it.

I posted on Instagram every day, and because I'd already practiced communicating my ideas for years, I got really good at it. I invested in the tools to help me grow, and within four months I reached 10,000 followers. I also did a full-day photoshoot with visual storytelling strategist and photographer John DeMato, complete with fourteen outfit changes. Later, I did two additional shoots—and I ended up using those photos for almost nine years.

I was all in. I remember one night hanging out with friends, a little tipsy and feeling bold, when I realized what I was doing: I was *Manufacturing Fame.*

I didn't get a big break, and I didn't have any special "in" with someone famous. I simply started doing the things that people who seemed famous to me were already doing. I figured that if I kept doing those things long enough, what was the real difference between them and me?

It worked because most of my competitors weren't willing—or able—to do it. It required consistent, focused effort every single day. By that point, we were making enough money from our Brandups that I had the time and space to commit to it, even though it didn't lead to many direct clients for a long stretch. But that wasn't the goal. I already had a strong referral network and plenty of people who knew me, knew what I did, and who I served. This work was about staying visible and building authority—writing thoughtful emails a couple of times a week and showing up consistently for the people already in my world.

All of these efforts kept me top of mind with my network

and with people who had seen me speak. More importantly, it made me look like someone who was doing something worth paying attention to. Someone with a point of view, and momentum. That made referrals easy. People could casually say, "You should check out Pia's book," or "You should follow Pia Silva on Instagram—she shares great stuff." And anyone I met during that time was effortless to follow up with. I always had something relevant to point them to—a book, a crash course, a piece of content—without it feeling salesy.

This was only sustainable with *systems*. I built my visibility the same way I worked with clients: in Intensives. I used software that let me schedule and recycle content across Instagram, Facebook, Twitter, and LinkedIn, so I wasn't constantly creating from scratch. In real life, people would tell me, "I see you everywhere," assuming I was posting all day, every day. What they didn't see was that most of that content had been created in a handful of focused Intensive sessions. I've *never* been someone who logs into Twitter (technically X, but it will always be Twitter), yet people were seeing me tweet three times a day.

This let me spend my time on what I'm actually good at and enjoy: generating thoughtful content. Communicating big ideas simply. Creating frameworks, branded concepts, and ways to make sense of the overwhelming world of business and how to build one. It's demanding, brain-heavy work, but developing those ideas forced me to understand them more deeply. Writing forced me to explain and clarify ideas I may have previously only understood in my gut.

Over time, that authority content built a larger audience and eventually began attracting new, cold leads—but that took *years*. In the meantime, it did something just as valuable: it nurtured the relationships I was *already* building through referrals. It kept me top of mind, kept my pipeline full of ideal clients, and gave me the leverage to keep raising my prices.

The AI Shift

Fast forward about seven years and content marketing began to change *fast* with AI. All of a sudden, early adopters were learning how to generate content much faster. Within a year, AI went from helping you create your content faster, to creating decent content in your voice, to generating entire videos *of* you just from a photo! And it's only getting better, and at an accelerated pace.

At first, this felt exciting. In theory, anyone could now do what I had done—build visibility and authority—but in a fraction of the time. I used to send podcast episodes to a transcription service, then manually turn those transcripts into blog posts and social content. Now, I could drop a podcast link into a tool and have it write the article for me. Seconds later, it could slice that same content into platform-specific posts, ready to publish.

Work that once took me hours—and systems I had refined over years—could suddenly be done with a single click.

At first, this felt like a win. I love efficiency and doing more in less time, and this was efficiency on steroids.

But it didn't take long to see the downside. Creating content used to have a real barrier to entry. You had to work with clients, test ideas, learn what actually worked, and *earn* your perspective. Once that barrier disappeared, anyone—even people who had *never worked with a single client*—could publish polished content and talk about their "ideas" as confidently as someone with years of real experience. Almost overnight, the ability to manufacture fame lost its value.

That's also why having a book used to matter so much. Not everyone could have one. Even a bad book required time, effort, and commitment. Suddenly, AI made it possible to "write" a book in a matter of hours. I'll never forget a friend canceling plans because he was up all night finishing his book with AI. He started and finished it in *one night.*

So what did this mean for me? Let's reach into my Econ 101 textbook: when supply explodes and demand stays the same—or drops—prices fall. In this case, the price wasn't money. It was perceived value.

As soon as everyone could do it—and so many people did—it stopped being so valuable.

That's why there's so much noise online with so little value. Reach is down—friends of mine with 100,000+ followers were suddenly barely getting any reach on their posts. Our inboxes are flooded with marketing. Email is still one of the best ways to stay in front of your audience, but it's way noisier than it once was because AI can write all your emails for you with one click.

So what does this mean for content marketing?

AI has created the illusion that things are easier and faster, when the opposite is true. Yes, it was a lot of work for me to build authority before AI, but I had the benefit of doing it in a world where just showing up was more than most people were willing to do. Today, that advantage is gone. For anyone starting now, the mountain is infinitely harder to climb if you want to use online content to generate new leads.

Because when *everyone* can publish effortlessly, how do you stand out and get noticed?

People *are* still successfully growing online audiences from scratch right now—but success to cold audiences is far more about vibes, entertainment, and being fun to watch, and less about depth, nuance, or real expertise. That's not a game everyone wants to play, or should. For high-level expert businesses, it's much harder for cold traffic to recognize what you actually know through content alone.

What used to work—building a content machine and putting it on autopilot—has become so inefficient that the time-to-benefit ratio is often not worth it unless you *already* have an audience.

Almost.

Content marketing isn't dead, but using it to attract high-quality clients from *cold* traffic is a lot harder than people want to admit. If you run a service business based on real expertise, and work with a small number of high-paying clients, social media is rarely the fastest or most reliable way to fill your pipeline.

What works better looks a lot like how I used content from 2013 to 2016.

Back then, almost everyone on my email list came from a real-life connection. I met them at events, through networking, or because they heard me speak on tiny stages—sometimes to rooms with just a handful of people. That list was built by hand, one conversation at a time.

And that's the good news! Anyone can do this, no social media savvy required. Using this strategy alone, we did $500,000 in sales from mid-2014 to mid-2015. Every one of those sales came from real-world connections paired with twice-monthly emails and blog posts. Nothing else.

That story is more relevant *now* more than ever. We're all overwhelmed by the things vying for our attention online, in our inboxes, in our text messages. Authority content still works, but not for the reason most people think. It's not about attracting strangers. It's about nurturing the real people you meet into referral partners and clients.

Think of content as part of your marketing ecosystem, not the whole thing.

When I was writing those early blog posts, I made a very intentional, and maybe even defiant, decision not to write for SEO. At the time, optimizing for SEO meant forcing keywords into your H1 and H2 headers and stuffing unnatural phrases throughout the article. You had to write a certain way, and it never felt right to me.

We were Worstofall Design, and we were about Badass Branding. Everything I believed was that you had to *be your brand* in everything you did. Content stuffed with keywords? Not badass. Dreadfully generic, actually.

I wrote creative, edgy articles because that was our brand voice. I wasn't writing to be found by cold traffic. I was writing for the organic traffic I generated simply by showing up in the world.

I knew it was working when people reached out and told me they'd been on my email list for months, sometimes years, always knowing they'd hire us when they were ready. Others said they'd gotten lost in my blog, loved everything I wrote, and by the time they contacted us, they were already set on working together.

The content wasn't designed to lure strangers to our site. It existed to turn curious people into clients. It made the sales process *easy* because the content did the selling for me. By the time someone reached out for a fit call, they were *already sold*. They loved what I had to say, how I said it, and they wanted some of that for themselves.

So how does this apply more than ten years later, when the marketing world has been flipped upside down multiple times and continues to change at an accelerating pace?

Because the thing that worked then still works now: *human relationships and trust.*

Instead of trying to compete in an online fight for attention that requires endless testing and optimization, reset your expectations. That path is only worth pursuing if you genuinely want to become an exceptional marketer or if you're trying to build a business that depends on massive audience growth.

But if you're reading this book, I'm guessing that's not your immediate goal.

Luckily, your current business can generate the life and income you want *without* relying on cold traffic or massive content output. Yes, you still need to market; every business does. But if you plan to invest seriously in authority content, you must *first* have a referral marketing machine in place that reliably feeds you leads, supported by a system you're committed to running consistently.

Too many people dive into authority content before that

foundation exists. Content creation demands a huge amount of time and energy, and when they ignore their referral engine, leads eventually dry up. They end up working harder than ever on content that isn't producing results, only to abandon it so they can scramble to find clients again. That feast-or-famine loop is exhausting, unnecessary, and entirely avoidable when you focus first on building and maintaining a strong referral marketing process.

Don't get me wrong—authority content is valuable for turning curious people into clients that are easy to close. When you meet them, they're referred to you, or they hear you on a podcast, on a stage, or in a workshop, your content will help them decide if they want to work with you.

Plus there's another reason for creating content without expecting cold traffic: it actually helps you *become* the authority you want to be seen as. The more you write and explain your thinking, the more *you* understand what you know.

I've coached a lot of people on building authority online, and I've seen a wide range of people with experience and expertise do it. It can be hard to write really great authority content even if you're a genuine expert in your field, because it's one thing to be good at what you do, and it's another thing to share what you know in a compelling and digestible way.

Shift in Thinking: Relationships Before Reach

Your marketing goal is simple: clear out the mental distractions of all the *coulds* and *shoulds*, choose *one* focused path, and consistently nurture the people who already want to see you win.

Marketing only feels overwhelming when you're trying to do everything at once. Success comes from showing up consistently with a clear message, a focused strategy, and a strong network of people who know, like, and trust you.

Referrals remain the fastest and most reliable path to high-quality clients because they shortcut most of the marketing process. Your relationships are what make your expertise visible, memorable, and referable.

Rather than stressing about building an online following to attract cold traffic, focus on building your referral engine first. It will bring in clients sooner and teach you what kind of content actually matters. Create content initially to deepen trust with your real-life connections and establish your authority there. If and when you choose to amplify it to cold traffic, you'll have the stability and confidence to sustain it.

Kelly O'Connell, the creative force behind the brand shop Kind & Funny, is proof that you don't need authority content to build a highly successful business.

Kelly joined us right as she was starting her business, meaning she had no audience, no platform, and no backlog of content. What she did have was a commitment to staying in touch. She consistently reached out to people in her existing network simply to connect.

Kelly comes across as outgoing, but she identifies as an introvert, someone who loves people and also needs space and downtime to recharge. That matters, because many introverts assume relationship-based marketing will exhaust them or feel inauthentic. Kelly shows what's possible when you approach outreach with care for your energy and no hidden agenda. Her goal was never to pitch. It was to stay present, thoughtful, and visible in people's lives.

Within six months, that approach led to her first $20,000 month, entirely from personal connections.

Since then, she's continued to show up consistently to deepen those relationships. One of her 1KOs is hosting monthly craft nights at her home, gatherings that leave people creatively energized and quietly reinforce her positioning as a true creative, someone you'd trust to build your brand and website.

That foundation has grown into a business that gives her real freedom. She works with clients she genuinely enjoys, brought her husband into the business so he could leave his job, and expanded her work into personal styling alongside branding. Just as importantly, she's designed a life that prioritizes creativity, fulfillment, and time.

As her 40th birthday approached, she was influenced by our community's focus on building a business that supports the life you actually want. She decided to rent a *literal castle* in the French countryside and invite more than twenty close friends for a weeklong celebration. Asking for help to make it happen was uncomfortable, but she did it anyway. She came back more confident, fulfilled, and clearer than ever about what success really means to her.

This is the point!

Everyone's No BS business will look different, shaped by who you are and what you value. The real work, and the real opportunity, is giving yourself permission to imagine what's possible for *you* and building toward it with intention.

Take Action:

1. **If you had to explain what you do to someone at a party in one sentence, what would you say? Write it down now.** Would it make someone immediately think of a specific person who needs you? Or does it sound like everyone else? Be honest. If it's the latter, you don't have a visibility problem. More leads won't help you. You've got a messaging problem, and you need to get clearer—stat.
2. **List 5-10 people who are well-connected to your ideal clients. Next to each name, write when you last spoke with them.** Make the list. Then look at the dates. If it's been more than a couple of months, you're letting your best referral sources go cold. Reach out to them, either to reconnect, invite them to something, or just to let them know you thought of them.
3. **Identify one idea from this chapter. Describe specifically how you can use it to keep in touch with your network while saving time.** If it's a low-lift event, pick a date, put it on the calendar right now, and invite 5 people. Stop overthinking it. What's the worst thing that could happen? Nobody shows up, and you're exactly where you are now. What's the best thing that could happen? You start to build the referral engine that changes your business!

If You Only Take One Thing From This Chapter:

You don't need a bigger audience; you need a stronger network. Stop trying to be everywhere online and start building real relationships with people who already know, like, and trust you—or who are one conversation away from it. Pick one strategy (your 1KO), commit to it, and show up consistently. That's how you build a pipeline of referrals you can rely on.

PART 2: NO BS MARKETING

PART THREE

No BS Sales

I'll never forget the time I was at a Business Network International (BNI) meeting and a woman stood up to give her 60-second elevator pitch and cited her services at $1,000/hour.

At the time, we were charging $65/hour, and I thought that was a decent rate since we started at $30/hour. $1,000/hour sounded ridiculous! What value could she possibly offer at that rate?

It also intrigued me. I thought to myself: *She must have something to offer if she values her time that highly.*

It made *quite* an impression on me. I used her as an example in my conversations with Steve as we continued to raise our prices and help our clients raise theirs. Her audacity in charging that rate conveyed a confidence that inspired me.

Maybe it will inspire you, too. If you want to be hired as an expert, it's important that you are viewed as one from the moment someone first interacts with you and your brand. Every cue you give them needs to be positioned and reinforced with expert framing.

How do we know someone is an expert at what they do? Here are a few cues:

1. They communicate the value they offer with confidence and clarity.
2. They're discerning about who they work with and are clear that they aren't just looking to work with anyone.
3. They're discerning about the projects they take on, and will only work with clients they can actually help (not just whoever will pay them).
4. They value their time.

Unfortunately, the way most service providers pitch their work fails to communicate points 2, 3, and 4 because they use one of two approaches.

The first is a menu of services with prices, available on a website or as a PDF sent to prospects. The second is a custom proposal based on what the prospect says they need, with a price calculated by multiplying estimated hours by an hourly rate. The final price may be variable or fixed, but it is still based on estimated hours.

Both of these approaches undermine the expertise you are trying to communicate.

A menu of services encourages prospects to shop the way they might shop for milk or eggs. If the same organic milk is ten dollars in one store and six dollars across the street, most people will buy the six-dollar gallon. Similarly, whether you're selling a logo or an hourly coaching package, prospects immediately compare prices. If one coach sells ten sessions for $2,000 and another sells ten sessions for $1,000, prospects focus on the price. They may not choose the cheapest option, yet they are unlikely to choose the most expensive one without a strong reason.

Custom proposals send their own signals. They may look thoughtful and tailored, but they're usually built entirely around what the *client* says they want. And while clients can describe their problems, they're not experts in the *solution*, which is why building a proposal solely around their stated needs often misses the mark. If they already knew exactly what to do, they wouldn't be hiring you! Their requests are often incomplete, misinformed, or disconnected from the deeper strategic issues they can't yet see.

Here are two examples.

One of my clients, Nicole Wells, coaches people who want to hone their presentation skills and speaking technique. Her clients expect that means giving them instructions on where to stand and how to project, but Nicole knows that becoming a great speaker goes much deeper than learning how to project your voice or eliminate nervous habits. Public speaking really isn't just about being on stage; it's about *all* our day-to-day meetings, work conversations, calls, etc., whether we are leading or participating. To truly help her clients, she needs to uncover the subconscious fears that shape how they communicate. She needs to help them discover who they are at their best so they can embody that version of themselves on stage.

She could sell a few sessions to teach tactics, but as an

expert, she knows that thriving on stage requires working on more than what her clients *think* they need. If she only focused on surface-level fixes, such as where to stand, how loud to speak, and how to relax your face, clients might see short-term improvement. Physical shifts do help, because changing the body can temporarily quiet the mind.

Yet without addressing what's actually driving the fear, the relief doesn't last. The nervous system is still running the same story underneath: *If I mess this up, I'll look stupid. If I look stupid, I'll lose respect. If I lose respect, everything falls apart.*

That fear shows up as rambling, freezing, or self-judgment, even when the person is objectively communicating clearly. So while they might technically have the skill, it doesn't land. When they don't get the feedback they're hoping for, people tend to fill in the silence with imagined judgment. And when that fear hasn't been identified or addressed, physical techniques start to feel like a performance, reinforcing the belief that their natural way of communicating isn't enough.

When Nicole goes deeper, the results are different. One client came in carrying a constant stream of negative thoughts about his abilities. Once they named it, they could play with it. Nicole challenged him to change that judgmental inner voice into something ridiculous, like Scooby-Doo, which immediately stripped it of its power. Over time, that shift changed how he felt in meetings, and his confidence followed.

Another client discovered that the real issue wasn't her authority at all, but a manager projecting their own style onto her. Months later, she landed a new role where her communication skills were the reason she was hired.

That's the difference between giving someone tactics and helping them resolve what's actually holding them back. One is temporary. The other changes how they show up everywhere, long after the engagement ends.

A second example I commonly see is when clients tell me they "just" need a new website. When I ask why, they typically say theirs is outdated and they want something more modern.

If that were really the issue, they could hire someone on Upwork to update it for a few hundred dollars. That is rarely the full situation. People start thinking about investing in a new website because something in their *business* is not working the way they want. They *think* the website is the problem. What they don't know, but the expert knows, is that a fresh website alone will not fix the deeper issue.

What they often need is a combination of retooling their messaging, positioning, brand design, offers and even how their website is laid out. That's not just a new website; it's a reimagining of how they present and market themselves and their business. The new website is an outer expression of all of that.

Now, back to the proposals.

We have a client who expressed a surface need, and the expert in you knows they need more. Yet the default way of pitching to them, and the way I see most service providers do it, is to price out the cost of what they are asking for. In Nicole's case, that would have previously involved charging per session, or in the second example, the cost to redo their existing website, adding a few updates so it feels new.

Let's say it's you writing a proposal for the requested website. You write a proposal that fits their budget and is comparable to the other quotes they received, and they say yes. You build them a new website, get paid, and they may even be happy with it.

But what *won't* happen?

They won't get the help they *actually* need, so they won't get the results they were seeking. They may not have even *expressed* these results to you, and perhaps you didn't position yourself as an expert to ask. Yet they were expecting them, whether they realized it or not. Instead of helping them uncover those goals, you took their request at face value and fulfilled it. You operated like an order taker, not an expert advisor, and you will get paid like one too.

There is nothing wrong with being an order taker, but order takers deliver limited value and therefore can't charge premium prices.

Plus, there is always going to be another order taker around the corner who will undercut your price. If you find yourself constantly having to justify your price to prospects, it's likely because they view your services as a commodity and are comparing them to other order-takers.

Yet the real issue is this: you aren't helping the client get what they want! You're staying surface-level, delivering superficial outcomes instead of value.

And look, everyone starts out this way. I started this way too! You cannot become an expert advisor without experience and knowledge. But at a certain point, as your understanding about your industry and your clients grows, you will get more skilled at assessing what your clients *really* need and want.

If you want to build a No BS business full of profit, freedom, and ease, there is a path forward for you. You can wield that knowledge into value-based offerings that deliver much deeper value than simply what your non-expert clients tell you they want.

I will never forget an expert interior designer we rebranded years ago. She explained that unlike most designers, she preferred to come in during the building or remodeling phase and work directly with the architects and general contractors. She was not just there to make the space pretty *after* it was built. She was there to customize the design from the ground up to match her client's needs and lifestyle.

That meant getting to know how her clients lived so she could advise on the details that matter: the exact height and depth of kitchen cabinets to make cooking effortless, outlet placement that hides cords and eliminates extension cables, built-in storage in surprising places that maximizes the space.

Her service is highly premium and designed for a very discerning clientele, yet even they would not always know what was possible, or how much more functional and beautiful their home could be if she were involved earlier in the process. She is a perfect example of bringing a level of thinking and expertise that the average person would never consider.

I think of her often, especially every time I wrestle with an ill-placed outlet or walk into a kitchen where the dishwasher door blocks the utensil drawer. She brings a deeper level of knowledge and expertise to her work and is someone who, back to the four points above, communicates her value confidently and clearly, is discerning about who she works with and the projects she takes on (meaning she works only with those clients who she knows she can help), and who truly–unapologetically–values her own time.

The good news is, you can do it too. The No BS Model for being seen and hired as an expert is a method I have installed in hundreds of clients' businesses and taught to thousands of students. It is called The Lead Product Method.

The Lead Product Method™ Explained

The Lead Product Method (LP) is a sales system that replaces the default free proposal process with **a paid first step**. It's a process I developed over years of working with clients, tweaking and adjusting over time. Though the words that are written in the brief are different, the basic framework is always the same. This process has proven, time and again, to close better-fit clients at higher prices with more ease.

I'll share the exact details with you on how it works. First, let me explain 10 reasons *why* it works.

1. It communicates that your time is valuable, while saving you time.

While most of your competitors rush off to write free proposals filled with deliverables, timelines, and even bits of strategy, you take a different approach. You tell the prospective client that you cannot write a proposal without first going much deeper into their business. They may believe they need a five-page website, but until you understand their business model, their audience, their offers, their goals, and the real challenges they are facing, you cannot create a website that will actually help them get customers. Developing that plan requires real expertise, which is why you charge for it. In comparison, the people offering free proposals for a generic five-page website suddenly look inexperienced and a little desperate.

And you should communicate that your time is valuable, because *it is!* A profitable expertise-based business is built on smart time management. You must spend your precious, limited hours on the highest-value actions, and marketing and sales will always take a meaningful share because they drive the entire business.

So the real question becomes: where should that time be invested?

The traditional way of pitching consumes an enormous amount of hidden, unpaid work. No matter how your leads come in, once someone expresses interest, the old model pushes you into multiple meetings, a custom proposal, and long follow-ups. Then, if the client does not close, every hour you spend pitching them disappears into the void. None of that time compounds or builds a long-term asset for your business.

Charging for the first step eliminates that waste. Your one-on-one time is narrowed down to a short fifteen-minute Fit Call. There are no second or third meetings because anything more requires going deeper into the problem and beginning to create solutions, which is the purpose of the LP itself.

You can then redirect that saved time into high-leverage activities like nurturing relationships, expanding your referral network, and increasing demand. One strong referral partner who trusts you can send you multiple clients over time. That is a far better return on your time than investing hours into each individual prospect, especially when a paid LP closes your ideal clients at a much higher rate.

2. It communicates you have a proven process.
When you spot that a prospect has a problem you can solve, and you present a clear and repeatable next step, it sends an immediate signal that you have done this before. When people hire an expert, they are really hiring the *promise* of what that expert knows and can do for them. This requires a certain amount of trust upfront because, unlike when you can try on a pair of pants in a store before *buying* them, hiring an expert means you do not get to see or "try on" the result until the very end, well *after* you've paid.

Since clients cannot see the results before they buy, they need something else to go on. They must *trust* that you can deliver. One of the most effective ways to communicate that trust is by having a structured process or framework. It signals expertise simply by demonstrating that you have done this many times before and have proven thinking and results behind your work. It also calms clients by making the unknown of working with you feel more predictable and dependable. And it taps into what is known as the Halo Effect: when someone seems skilled in one area, we naturally assume they are skilled in others too. A clear process builds that trust quickly.

3. You cut the line in front of your competition.
We live in a world of instant gratification, and people with problems want solutions quickly. When you clearly identify the problems you can solve, and offer an immediate first step, at

a no-brainer price, it's often far more compelling than lengthy proposals for high-priced, long-term engagements. I can't tell you how many times I sold a Lead Product to someone who was in the middle of collecting proposals from other design agencies, simply because I gave them a way to move into solution mode instead of staying stuck in the purgatory of comparing similar options from a sea of designers.

4. It positions you as an expert and increases the value of your advice to the client.
Would you ever expect Tony Robbins to pitch you for free? Of course not. He's in high demand and his time is valuable. You might not be Tony Robbins status yet, but that same logic applies. When you admire someone, or view them as a true authority, you don't expect them to offer multiple free calls or sessions. You naturally assume they have plenty of paying clients lined up. This is the subtle message a paid first step sends to your prospects. It signals that your time is valuable and that people pay to access your expertise.

Plus people value what they pay for. Notice how differently you show up when you've paid for something versus when it's free. You're more likely to be on time, stay engaged, and actually see it through. The simple act of paying changes how seriously your brain treats the information.

I've watched this dynamic play out for more than 15 years. When someone pays me thousands of dollars for advice, they almost always take action on it (and therefore get results.) What's interesting is that I don't reserve that advice only for paying clients. I share it openly on my podcast, in my emails, blog articles and on social media, plus I often give the same guidance in casual conversations with other business owners. And yet, those people rarely act on it. Not because it has less value, but because free advice is easy to nod along to without ever fully committing to *doing* anything about it.

This is called the "endowment effect." We value what we pay for more than identical things we get for free. Once you pay, your brain wants to justify the expense—so it convinces you the thing is worth it. Stanford research backs this up: investment (time or money) triggers dopamine, which creates attachment. That's why free advice gets ignored and paid plans get action.

Bottom line: you can deliver the exact same strategic advice in a free proposal, but the client will place far more value on a paid version.

5. It builds trust fast.
Once a client pays you for this first step, they'll already value your advice more. Yet this Lead Product Method goes far beyond that. It builds trust quickly because it's centered around asking really good initial and follow up questions in order to understand the full picture of the client's needs, goals, and challenges.

The psychology is simple: true listening kicks off empathy and rapport, both of which build trust quickly. When you ask good follow up questions in a way that shows you *get* the client—not just what they said, but the fears and dreams behind it—they feel *seen* instead of sold to. That flips things in the relationship to where you're not *pitching* anymore; you're on their team helping to solve a puzzle. They've paid you, so now they're an open book, and they want to get to a real, authentic solution. When you ask questions that make them think about themselves or their business in a new way, they begin to see you as the *only* person they could work with, because you're the only person who has not only taken the time to understand them; your questions have given them the clarity they didn't even know they were lacking. Clients start leaning in for your advice because they feel understood. Trust builds quickly because you *earned* it by actually listening.

The Lead Product Method taps into a fundamental human truth: most people crave being seen and understood for psychological safety, connection, and well-being.

And once that trust is established, the client will be in a completely different mindset when considering the investment to work with you for the bigger project.

Since you've worked with clients before, you've probably had one of the following two things happen to you.

After you've been working with them for a while, they suddenly tell you in the middle or at the end of the project, when they're impressed with your work, that you should charge more.

That, or they start to give you more and more work once they get to know you and have had a good working experience with you.

Now imagine if they had that level of trust and faith in you *before* they needed to decide if they wanted to hire you?

The LP moves the trust that normally develops in the middle of a project to the very beginning. Yes, they pay a small fee for the LP, but what they originally came to you for was something much larger. Instead of pitching that full engagement when trust is still low, the LP lets you build trust first through a smaller initial experience. There is always some blind faith involved in hiring an expert whose results won't show up until later—and the LP positions you as the safest person to place that faith in now.

Imagine how different they'll feel when they finally *do* see your proposal for the larger engagement. If they barely know you, they judge your free proposal mostly on price and vibes. But after an eye-opening LP interview—and a thoughtful, strategic plan that shows them how what they *thought* they needed was incomplete, slightly off, or even wrong—everything shifts. Your recommendation is grounded in a real understanding of their situation. Your offer to take this off their plate feels like a *relief*. And the final number no longer feels like a cost; it feels like a small price to pay to put the problem in the hands of a trusted advisor who understands it better than anyone—including them.

6. The Lead Product increases the client's budget.
When Allison Sebastian, founder of South Square Creative, delivered her first Lead Product, she asked me what she should pitch at the end. The client only had a $3,000 to $5,000 budget, but her lowest package was $5,500. After the LP interview, it was clear that what the client *really* needed was her $8,000 package. I told her to use the brief to paint a picture of what her client really needed and what Allison could make possible for her, and offer her the package to match. The client ended

up buying the $8,000 package and didn't even mention the smaller offer.

When Paul Heaton, owner of The Comms Guru, delivered a Lead Product Brief for an internal comms project, the company originally said they only had the budget for his $3,000 offer. Once he delivered the Lead Product, they realized they really wanted, and needed, the $12,000 offer and they closed without issue.

And when Aga Siuda, owner of *Graphroots Design*, delivered her first Lead Product to a nonprofit, they loved the brief and wanted to hire her—yet she quickly learned the board *required* a Request for Proposal (RFP) process to open candidacy to others. The program lead actually asked her if they could use her brief as the outline for the RFP! Though that request was a little frustrating, she had been paid for the brief and acquiesced. Once they received the submissions, they came back to Aga and said they wanted to hire her for $32,000, even though she came in as the *top* bid. I think it's safe to say that without the LP there is *no way* this organization would have chosen the most expensive option after an RFP process.

I hear this time and again from students who learn the Lead Product Method: clients say they have one budget, and then it goes out the window once they go through the LP process.

That's because the budgets clients initially have when they come to you is what I call the "Fear Budget." If you ask a client what their budget is, do you *really* think they are going to tell you how much they are willing to spend? Would you? What if you say a number that's higher than the person was going to charge you? You'd end up paying more for no reason!

Any budget a client cites upfront is usually generated from a scarcity mindset that is focused on spending *as little as possible*. And that makes sense, because until they have clarity on what the actual outcome might be from the engagement, and the value they are going to receive, it's just money *spent*. Not an investment to get a future result.

Once they can see what opportunities they are going to gain, and what benefits they'll experience by making the investment, the amount of money they're willing to invest is much higher.

A simple example: what if I invited you to a party and I told you the tickets are $1,000. Would you immediately say yes? I mean, you like parties, it sounds like fun, but $1,000? You can go to free parties, and it's not clear why this party would be worth $1,000.

Now what if I invited you to the same party for $1,000, but I told you there would be five perfect clients there that I would introduce you to, all of whom already told me they need your help, and all of whom definitely have the money to invest in your highest priced services that are $20,000+.

Now how does that $1,000 feel to you? I'd pay double or triple or more to go to that party. That $1,000 was a *cost* when it was just a party. Now it's an *investment* that can potentially generate up to $100,000 in clients, maybe even more if I meet more people there.

It's not necessary to quantify the exact financial return your clients can expect; you just need to be clear that there's an outcome versus merely a process/deliverables. Whether it's helping your clients attract more customers, close them more easily, charge them more money, feel more confident, communicate more effectively to get what they want, experience more contentness, happiness, or joy—the moment the investment in working with you stops being about the *deliverables,* and starts being about the *outcome,* is when the fear budget goes out the window.

Sometimes the "fear budget" sticks around even after the LP. That's usually because you skipped a step: you didn't properly qualify them, you didn't build enough trust during the engagement, or you didn't dig deep enough to uncover their real motivations and tie your work to them.

7. The LP demonstrates discernment and your commitment to solving actual problems.

Part of the reason most people "hate sales" and are scared to be salesy is that we have all been on the other side of a slimy sales conversation. You know what I'm talking about: the kind where someone is trying to *convince* you to buy something. It feels that way because you don't really want, or think you need, whatever they're offering you. Because it feels so uncomfortable to be in that position, we want to avoid putting other people in that position. On the other hand, when you can tell the person you are speaking to is *not* trying to sell you, but instead, is truly trying to figure out if they can even help you, our shoulders can relax. If you tell someone "hey, I need a five-page website, please quote me a price," and they say "hold on a second, tell me a little more about what you are trying to do, and what you are hoping to achieve. In my experience, sometimes a new website might not even be necessary," it can be immediately disarming.

Because *most* people will respond by giving a quote, asking about your budget, and offering to write a proposal, the person who says "wait a second, let's figure out if you even really need it," is immediately different. It feels like they are *on your side*—and they are looking out for you. They aren't trying to sell you a website just because you said you want one; they want to make sure they can actually *help* you before they even begin to talk numbers.

This demonstrates, through your actions rather than your words, that you're not interested in selling to anyone with money in their pocket. You're committed to working only with people you can truly help, and walking away when your work isn't the right fit.

I've stopped a lot of people in their tracks by slowing the conversation down and asking more questions about what the real challenges are. If by the end of the conversation it's clear they're very new to business, aren't in a position to invest, and probably don't have enough experience to make the investment worthwhile at this point, I will point them in a different direction. Meaning, I will tell them they shouldn't invest the amount that I charge right now, because they aren't in a position to fully benefit from it.

You build enormous goodwill when you tell someone they *shouldn't* spend money with you right now. I've had those people come back when they're ready, and I've had them send referrals because they remember I didn't try to sell them when I could have.

This works because I'm not trying to "sell" anyone. I'm genuinely trying to discern if I can help them or not. When you approach every prospect with that mindset—even when you do offer the LP—the conversation feels authentic and the "salesiness" disappears.

8. You get *paid* for your strategic ideas.
Imagine you want to hire someone to decorate your home. You speak to two interior designers.

The first asks you to send photos and describe your style, then sends back a quote with a Pinterest moodboard for inspiration.

The second tells you she needs to see the space first and understand your vision. She asks for a small fee but promises you'll have a clear picture of what's possible—something you could even implement yourself if you want. You spend a couple of hours walking through your house together. She asks about each room: what you like and don't like, how you use the space, what your daily life looks like, what your family enjoys doing at home, ideas you've been considering, your personal style. Then she gives you a full workup of everything she'd upgrade and how it will make your home more functional, easier to maintain, and designed for the way you actually live.

Which designer would you trust to design your home?

When we pitch for free, we're usually giving away ideas because we think the client needs a taste of what we offer. We get specific about inputs, deliverables, timeline, and price—all to convince them to hire us.

The problem is, we're doing this on thin information. Either it's a shot in the dark—you're suggesting things without really understanding the client (like designer #1)—and you might get it terribly wrong. Or you take the time to gather enough information to make it somewhat informed. But even if you're giving brilliant value in your proposed plan, the client won't value it as much because they got it for free. Plus, you're giving away knowledge and ideas to someone with no obligation to pay you for them.

When they hire you, this free-pitching process seems to work. But when they don't—or worse, when they push back on your price or disappear—it takes a piece of your integrity with it. You gave them something valuable that you spent years learning, and it wasn't respected or paid for.

Sell those ideas. Make them *actually* informed and smart by taking clients through a proper process.

9. It scares away tire-kickers, who were never going to pay, and attracts the kinds of clients you want.
I remember offering someone the LP once, and his response was that he was interested, but "let's meet for coffee and discuss." I chuckled and said there really wasn't anything else to discuss. "Any discussion you want to have about your business, and so much more, is covered in the LP!" I later heard from a colleague that he had also asked them for multiple meetings, and a proposal, and ended up ghosting them.

He's what we call a tire kicker: someone who's willing to invest plenty of time shopping for free, but with no real intention of moving forward. Often, people don't even realize they're doing this. They think they're being thorough, and it's fun to imagine hiring someone to help them, yet they aren't committed to it. But with no skin in the game, changing their mind costs them nothing except time—which they may not value highly.

Requiring payment changes that dynamic instantly. It forces people to decide how serious they actually are—and in this case, holding that boundary saved me three hours and a pointless coffee meeting.

I saw this play out even more clearly at a paid workshop on creating paid workshops. Meta, I know. About fifty of us were working on our workshop titles. A few people shared theirs, and the instructor asked who would attend based on the title alone. Almost every hand shot up. Hypothetically, everything sounded amazing.

The following week, one participant—who had received rave feedback from that exact audience—launched her workshop and shared the ticket link.

Not one person who had raised their hand bought a ticket. *Not one.*

That's the difference between imagining a purchase and actually making one. Ask me if I would attend something, and my answer might be an enthusiastic *yes*. Ask for my credit card, and a different part of my brain takes over, and that answer is just as likely to be *no*.

Imagining buying something, and actually buying something, are completely different experiences. In theory, everything sounds great. In reality, asking for a credit card activates a very different part of the brain. Some people even enjoy collecting proposals or quotes because it lets them fantasize about solving the problem without having to act or spend money.

When you charge upfront, and someone pays you even a small amount, they're signaling a different level of commitment.

They're showing you they're ready to take action.

That's why you'll sometimes see online trainings priced at one dollar: far fewer people opt in, but the ones who do are demonstrating real commitment, and that changes everything.

10. The LP makes you stand out from your competitors.
Last but certainly not least, having a Lead Product immediately sets you apart from your competition. The moment you clearly lay out your process and explain how you know what a client needs, why this is the right first step, and how you solve problems like theirs, something shifts. Prospects can feel that they are dealing with a different caliber of expert.

You become more memorable. You become easier to refer to. And you stand out without trying to perform or convince.

Having a clear process puts people at ease. It signals that you're not trying to sell them just *anything*, but that you are leading them through a thoughtful, *proven* way of working. It communicates integrity. You are not trying to force any deal across the finish line; you only work with clients who are a true fit and whose problems you can *actually* solve.

That alone separates you from service providers who rely on free proposals, endless negotiation, and bending themselves into whatever shape it takes to make a sale.

The Lead Product in Action

Wanna get paid to build trust upfront so you can easily upsell into those big juicy projects?

Here's how The Lead Product Method works:

- **Step 1**: Hop on a 15-minute **Fit Call**.
- **Step 2**: If they're a good fit, offer them a small, paid engagement—your **Lead Product**.
- **Step 3**: If they say yes, conduct a **Lead Product Interview**, which is a deep dive. Ask smart questions. Listen. Uncover problems they didn't even know they had.
- **Step 4**: Deliver the **Lead Product Brief**, a short written brief that outlines *exactly* what they need (including the needs they didn't know they had), why they need it, and how to move forward—whether they hire you or not.
- **Step 5**: Host the follow up call that seamlessly moves them into the next step.

It's a simple process, and its success is all in the execution. Let's go over each step in detail.

Step 1: Fit Call - Genuine Curiosity

When I ask small business owners who their ideal clients are, there is one answer I get often: *people who understand the value of what I do and have the budget to pay for it.*

I'm always tickled by this answer—*sure, you and everybody else!*

This answer is often born out of frustration after countless conversations with prospective clients who don't understand your value or repeatedly push back on your pricing. When you're worn down by those experiences, price and resistance can start to feel like the whole problem, even when they're really just symptoms.

The problem is if that is the *only* prerequisite, you're not being discerning about who you work with. You aren't concerned about how much value *you* can provide, or if they are the kind of client you can deliver your *best* work for. You just want to make a sale wherever and to whomever you can.

And your prospects can feel it.

If you hate sales calls it might be because, deep down, you're on a sales call to sell the person. You're feeling needy, and they can tell. *Your sale* is more important to you than *their problem*. And it doesn't feel great for either of you.

Even if you aren't giving that needy energy, the way most people even take these calls sets it up to feel salesy. A discovery call, free consultation, or free strategy session is intended for *you to give free value* and then *hope* that they buy at the end. This is a mismatch of expectations: sending the message that you're just there to help for free, when you're really hoping they buy from you. They know they're there to be sold to, so their guard is up. Sometimes the move from giving free advice to "hey, maybe you should pay me for more of this" can get uncomfortable and hard to navigate.

That's why I started calling them Fit Calls. Because as someone who was *definitely* scared to come off as pushy or salesy, I would chat with people and offer up *loads* of free advice, hoping they would see my brilliance and ask how they could pay me. And when they didn't, I had a hard time bringing it up.

A Fit Call, on the other hand, completely reverses the positioning of the conversation. The whole point of the Fit Call is to see if we are a fit *for each other*. It both takes the pressure off the call—I'm trying to figure out if you're a fit for me, and I'm not going to sell you if you aren't—and makes it explicit that the point of the call is to get to the sale *only if it makes sense*.

Instead of being in opposition, where I am trying to sell you something and you are trying to hold onto your money, we are on the same team. We are collectively figuring out if I can help you, and we won't know until we talk.

As I said earlier, I find that people are much more open when they can tell that I am genuinely trying to understand who they are and what they need help with, and am ready to send them away if it's not a perfect match.

In order to run a successful Fit Call, we start with the premise that you are here to figure out if and how you can help someone, and *only if you can* will you suggest a way to work together.

This means you must be *super clear* on who would be a good fit for you, and who wouldn't. When you know what a great client looks like, as well as the warning signs for a bad fit, you'll know what specific questions to ask to suss this out.

Before I started doing this—when "anyone that would pay me" was a good fit—all I focused on was what they needed. Website? *Yes we do that!* Logo? *Absolutely, we do that too!* Social media profiles, lead magnets, naming? Before we had done all of those for clients, I still knew we technically *could*, so I said *yes*!

Anything to get the client.

Once I got clear on who was a great fit for us and who wasn't, the questions I asked changed. We worked with 1-3 person service businesses, built websites exclusively on Squarespace, and delivered projects in 1-3 day Intensives.

If someone told me their website was on WordPress, I didn't panic, I just dug in further. I asked how they got clients and how much traffic the site had. If their business ran on referrals and the site had very little traffic, they could still be a fit. We had successfully moved many clients from WordPress to Squarespace. But if their answer was SEO, organic search, and hundreds of blog posts driving leads, I would immediately say we were not the right partner. We don't design on WordPress, and I would never recommend a move that could jeopardize what was already working.

Another immediate red flag was ecommerce. We had done ecommerce sites before, yet they took more time and were harder to make profitable. We *could have* specialized in them and built a tighter process, but we chose service businesses instead. Specializing meant we could follow the same repeatable process for every client, which made the work more efficient and far more profitable.

Just because you *can* take on a project outside your specialty doesn't mean it's a good idea. Every exception pulls you further from the process you know works. Unless you're deliberately expanding into a new market, and are prepared to accept some unprofitable work as part of a longer-term strategy, sticking to your niche is almost always the more sustainable choice.

During the Fit Call, your job is to ask direct, specific questions to fully understand why they reached out, what they believe they need, the challenges they're experiencing, and the problems they want to solve. The purpose of the call is not to pitch, but to determine whether they are genuinely a strong fit for what you deliver and the way you work.

The exact questions you ask will be different from mine,

and the more Fit Calls you do and the clearer you get on who your ideal client really is, the more dialed-in those questions become. Most calls touch on the same basics: why someone reached out, what challenges they're dealing with, a bit of background, what they've tried before, and what they want to accomplish. The difference between your Fit Calls and mine is not just the questions themselves, it's what you're listening for in their answers.

Take Amin Astaneh, founder of *Certomodo*, a software reliability consultancy, as an example. Beyond understanding the technical situation, he listens for readiness. He pays attention to where the company is in its growth, the severity and frequency of incidents they have experienced, and whether there is genuine urgency behind the problem. He also notices how executives talk about their engineers, because his work succeeds only in organizations where trust and empathy exist. In other words, Amin is not just qualifying a project, he is also assessing whether the company is emotionally and structurally prepared to do the work required to get results. *If and only if* it is clear they are a perfect fit, does he move to the next part of the Fit Call and offer them his LP.

Step 2: Offer Your Lead Product

I started offering the LP because I hated pitching. Having a set process and product with a set price felt completely different—like when customer service says "sorry, company policy!" The decision isn't personal anymore.

Oh, you want to keep talking about your problems and pick my brain for free? Sorry, company policy. Gotta buy the LP.

It's a set price, a proven process, and a signal that your prospect is actually ready for solutions. It's not the entire solution, but it's a critical first step. How can you solve a problem you haven't thoroughly understood or planned for? You can't bake a cake without a recipe, build a house without a blueprint, or create a successful brand without first knowing the goal and making a plan to achieve it.

When you sell your expertise, you're also selling your approach to solving problems. There are other approaches out there (obviously subpar!), but you need to sell yours as the best one. And you can't do that until you fully uncover the problem and understand it from all angles.

Imagine walking into a doctor's office, saying you broke your foot, and they immediately send you upstairs for a cast—without examining you. It might be a sprain. But nobody would know because they didn't look hard enough upfront.

Here's where introducing the LP can get tricky: if you present it as a *detour* instead of the *direct path to solutions*, your prospect will say no. You need to connect the value of the LP to the problem and goals the client just told you they have.

Don't say: "You need a five-page website? Great! The first step is paying me to create your brand strategy. Brand strategy is important if you want a new website."

This erodes all the trust you just built. They told you they want a website. You tried to sell them brand strategy—something they didn't ask for. Plus, you didn't even quote the website. They're thinking: "I don't need brand strategy. I'll just go with the other designer who sent me a free proposal."

You and I both know that without clear brand messaging, a

new website won't help their business much. But they don't know that. They don't know what strategy even is, and they certainly don't want to pay extra for it.

Instead, meet them where they are. Draw a direct line from where they are now to the outcome they want.

Try this: "You need a new five-page website to attract and close more ideal clients? Great! That's exactly what we do. The next step is [your Lead Product], where we figure out exactly what this website needs to be to get you those ideal clients."

Figuring out what a website needs goes far beyond functionality. It requires clarity on how it should look, who it's speaking to, what it's offering, what language will resonate, and which pages are truly necessary. All of these decisions come from brand strategy—but you're framing them in a way that aligns with what the client already understands and is ready to engage with right now.

The LP needs to feel like one critical step *closer* to their goal, not a detour with a price tag attached.

Here are two more magical pieces to the offer that will make it an easy yes:

The price of the LP gets applied to the final project should they choose to hire you for the entire website; and

The LP is valuable on its own, so even if they don't move forward, they will still have received more value than they paid for and are one step closer to their goal.

Number one is crucial because it demonstrates that this is the first step in the process of their project, versus an addition or something unrelated. Unlike your competitors who are going to pitch them for a full $10,000 or $20,000+ website engagement at this point in the sales process, you're telling them to only pay you a little bit ($500 or $1,000, for example) to get started. It's an easier yes and it moves them closer to what they want, faster.

I always tell prospective clients that I've had many clients purchase only my LP, which I call *The Brandshrink*, without the intention of doing the full project, because it is valuable on its own. We want them to know this engagement is a valuable product, not simply a paid proposal your competitors are giving away for free.

(Of course, this means you need to *make* it a valuable product on its own, but I'll get to that shortly.)

When you position the Lead Product this way, the stars align. Let's say you build trust in the Fit Call and the prospect feels like you really hear their challenges. They see you're offering this LP because they are the exact kind of client you work with every day. If this is the case, it will go one of two ways:

Either they'll say an emphatic yes because they can't wait to start solving their problem.

Or they'll say they need to think about it, they aren't ready yet, they're just collecting information—or some other version of "not now."

Obviously you want the first scenario. When it happens—especially the first time—it feels magical. When you get that first excited yes and the person books and pays immediately, you'll realize that if you'd been writing free proposals, this conversation would have ended with you doing unpaid work and crossing your fingers. Instead, you just got paid. How fun!

If they don't buy on the spot, it usually means one of three things:

1. You could have asked better questions and listened more deeply so they felt heard instead of pitched to.

2. You could have connected the LP more explicitly to their stated goals, making it feel like a valuable next step rather than an extra expense.

3. Or they were window shopping (whether they knew it or not) and aren't actually ready to solve their problem right now.

In the third scenario, celebrate. Instead of going on a fantasy ride with someone who'll happily take your time, ideas, and free work while dangling payment somewhere in your future, you got in and out in 15 minutes. Reinvest that saved time into nurturing your network and bringing in your next prospect.

Step 3: The Lead Product Interview

When you were a child, was there a special adult in your life who really listened to you? Maybe a parent, grandparent, teacher, or family friend who asked questions, gave you their full attention, and made you feel important. You could tell they cared because they didn't just listen—they asked follow-up questions. They waited until they fully understood what was going on and how you felt before offering advice.

It's that feeling of being seen, heard, and understood that all humans crave. It makes us feel like we matter.

That fundamental need is why the live Lead Product interview is so powerful.

Wherever I teach this process, people inevitably ask if they can send an intake form instead of interviewing live. I say *resist*. The magic of the LP interview is in the live gathering of information and allowing the client to be heard.

The Lead Product interview is a series of questions that give you a full, detailed understanding of your client's situation and goals. You want to understand where they are, where they've been, and where they're trying to go. What they've tried, what's worked, what hasn't. What they like and don't like. What success looks like to them—and then what success *really* looks like to them.

For example, they might first tell you success means "our tech stack is organized and cheaper." But if you dig deeper, you'll uncover that success *really* means "we're saving time, money, and energy that we can reinvest in our business and our lives."

Your questions will vary depending on your expertise. Start with a list that uncovers the above, then build in space to be curious and ask as many follow-up questions as possible. Imagine yourself a detective figuring out the full picture. If something confuses you, stay confused and ask questions until you get clarity. This is not the time to explain things—it's time to listen with the aim to understand. This can be hard for people used to listening only long enough to take their turn speaking (we're all guilty). But real listening is a critical skill in the Lead Product interview—and a powerful one in life.

As you do more interviews, you'll continually hone your questions. Grab my top 30 questions at scalesolobook.com/resources as a jumping-off point, then adapt them for your clients. Every time you finish a project and realize you could have used more information, add that question to your list. This document will evolve as you get better and work with more clients. Your questions should evolve with you.

Try to say as little as possible during the interview. The value comes from the client thinking out loud as they answer your questions and from your thoughtful follow-ups. Great questions help clients see their challenges and opportunities more clearly than just giving them the answer. That's how our brains work—generating answers yourself builds stronger neural pathways than passively receiving information. What you're really doing is learning together.

If you do this well, it will set you apart. Most experts lead with the value they have to offer. They want to share *their* ideas and solutions. They think they need to lead with information to help people. What could be more helpful than giving someone the exact information they need?

But true experts want to understand *first*—not only so your advice is truly applicable, but so it lands with the client. Newbie Lead Product interviewers often start explaining ideas as soon as they understand the situation. This is understandable, but *resist*. I have to make a real effort not to start explaining things. I'm a natural teacher and I love it. But it's always more powerful when I don't.

When I do this well, clients tell me at the end of the interview how much clearer they are—and I barely said anything. They experience clarity because they discovered it themselves, not because I explained it to them.

When people use this process for the first time, they're often stunned by how effective it is. They feel more energized about the work, clients gain clarity about their real challenges, and there's no ambiguity about next steps. Most importantly, it reveals a gap between what the client initially asked for and what they truly need—something that rarely surfaces in a traditional sales conversation.

This is huge because it reveals how the original client request wouldn't actually solve their problem. That's when my students tell me they can't believe they were ever pitching without this process.

I love when students share that their client was thankful at the end of the interview—even before receiving any recommendations.

Jacob Kleinman Phillips, the brains and heart behind Touchpoint Design, experienced this when a prospect came to him for a "simple new logo." Since he'd just learned the LP method, he offered her the LP instead.

The LP uncovered what her business *really* needed to succeed and why she deserved to invest in herself right now to chase her dreams. She bought his $12,500 branding and website package—his highest-priced project to that point. She'd initially admitted she'd never spent this kind of money on her business before. This was the biggest objection he needed to overcome, and the LP turned it into an enthusiastic yes without pushback on price.

Step 4: The Lead Product Brief

When you leave an LP interview, sometimes you and the client are crystal clear on what needs to happen. Other times, it feels like a thousand puzzle pieces were just dumped on the table and you need quiet time to piece them together. Either way, organize all the findings and recommendations into a tangible deliverable—something that paints a clear, exciting picture of what's possible and exactly what they need to do next.

This is the Lead Product Brief. If you've written strategy documents or proposals before, you might think you know what this should look like.

After seeing hundreds of briefs from people I've taught—especially their first ones—I can safely say I've never seen anyone write a brief in this particular framework.

The Lead Product Brief needs to hit a few chords right to really sing. Give lots of value, but not so much you overwhelm the client. Give detailed examples, but don't actually do the work yet. Make sure they feel heard and understood, but don't overwhelm them with every detail they shared. Solve their problems as much as possible, but focus primarily on the problems you solve through your expertise.

The Lead Product Brief's goal is to make your potential client feel connected and inspired by the vision you lay out, and clear on how the plan connects to their big goals. Bring their vision to life so clearly they can practically see it. When that happens, they'll see you as the *only* person who can deliver it.

Step 5: The Follow Up Call

This brings us to the final step: transitioning into the close. This call is positioned as an important follow-up to the brief, where the client can ask questions, react to what they read, and request changes if anything feels off. The purpose is to make sure you both agree the brief reflects the right direction and for the client to decide if they'll move forward with you on the larger engagement. If you've done Steps 1–4 well, this won't feel like selling. It will feel like a natural continuation of the work you've already done together.

Your job on this call is to confidently guide them toward a clear decision and make the next step feel obvious and easy. That means being prepared to show them exactly what happens next. Once they say yes, lock in the timeline on the call, explain what secures it, and outline what they can expect immediately after—contract, invoice, and onboarding details. Then follow through right away. No vague "I'll send next steps later." This moment sets the tone for the entire engagement. When clients know what's coming, feel taken care of, and experience you leading with clarity, the close doesn't feel heavy or awkward. It feels like a relief. And that's when people happily move forward.

How to Write an LP Brief that Upsells

Now you know the basics of the Lead Product Method. In this section, we'll go deeper into Step 4: the Lead Product Brief. I'm going to walk you through how to write one that upsells.

Part 1: Current Situation

It's tempting to dive straight into your advice, but taking a moment to set the stage makes your guidance far more effective. It puts the client in the right mindset and anchors them into the key details that matter. It also demonstrates deep understanding and creates space to ensure your assumptions are correct before you proceed.

A great Current Situation section is a few paragraphs max.

Give a high-level description of the client's business or life and briefly describe what they've been doing well. Summarize the main challenges they're facing and any specific events that contributed to those challenges. Then summarize their goals—not just what they want, but what getting those things will ultimately mean for them. Finally, wrap up with a transition line that positions what you're about to tell them as the key to achieving those goals.

Part 2: Findings and Recommendations
This is the meat of the brief, and it's your time to shine. Describe their most exciting opportunities and what they need to upgrade, change, or install to reach their goals. Imagine this is your best friend who came to you with a problem, and you get to tell them everything you know about fixing it. Don't hold back your plan or ideas—this is a paid engagement, and it's important you give real value, not just surface-level information as a carrot to the main project.

Whenever possible, go beyond telling them *what* they need. Give them specific examples to make this brief unique to them and their situation. One of the most common mistakes people make when first writing LP briefs is staying at the surface level—telling prospects what they need to fix without showing them what it looks like to fix it. They say things like: "You need a good logo," "You need consistency across touchpoints," "You need a color palette," or "You need a strong tagline." This is what I call "level one" thinking. It's generic advice you could give to anyone. It's safe, obvious, and ultimately, not very useful.

If you want your LP briefs to be truly strategic, you need to go deeper.

Instead of telling someone they need a consistent brand, you might say: "You need a brand that reflects the sassy, bold, unapologetic voice you have in person. When people meet you, you're confident, opinionated, and not afraid to offend. But your website sounds cautious and restrained. That disconnect is blocking your brand from attracting the same people who are instantly sold on you in real life."

It gets even better when you bring in specific references that immediately paint a picture. For example: "Your brand voice needs the sophistication of Meryl Streep with the sharp edge and humor of Sarah Silverman."

That kind of guidance gives the client something they can actually feel and envision. It's what gives them goosebumps and the excitement to move forward with you.

I learned this early when writing an LP brief for our client, Stash Wealth. They positioned themselves as contrarian in the financial services world, yet their messaging felt buttoned up and polite. In the brief, I wrote: "Instead of explaining that you're 'not your father's financial firm,' *stop being* your father's financial firm and say something like, 'Get your financial shit together.'"

That line became a cornerstone of their brand and marketing. I wasn't even pitching them copy, yet sharing that line allowed them to viscerally feel what their brand needed to sound and feel like. It captured the tone, attitude, and point of view they needed to own.

That's the difference between generic advice and real strategic insight.

Whenever it feels relevant, connect your recommendations explicitly back to the ultimate goals using "so that" statements.

For example, if you're outlining a social media strategy—such as spending 20 minutes commenting on LinkedIn before publishing a new post—close the section by tying it to outcomes: "This rhythm of engaging first and *then* posting increases reach and visibility, *so that* you consistently generate new leads and support your goal of signing two new clients each month."

Part 3: Summary Conclusion
Wrap up your recommendations with a paragraph summarizing the big opportunities you just laid out and how implementing this plan will get them to their desired goal.

Part 4: North Star
This section can look different depending on your services. I use it to document big foundational decisions that will make the project easier to implement. Because we're a branding agency, we state their target market, keywords for the brand, and a detailed outline of all the website pages we recommend. This gets the client to sign off on many decisions upfront and allows the proposal at the end to be even more specific and clear.

Part 5: Moving Forward Section
The brief ends with the proposal of what it will take to make this beautiful, thoughtful, inspiring plan come to life. The goal is to make this feel like the obvious next step. By the time your client reaches this last section, they should feel really clear on everything that needs to happen. It should feel like a no-brainer

when they see it all summed up in a list of deliverables with one fixed price attached.

A great Moving Forward section is not just a list of deliverables, but a description of how each deliverable will get the client an outcome they want. We do this using "so that" statements.

Instead of listing "Logo," we might say: "Design an iconic, timeless logo that will stand out on promotional products so that you stay top of mind for your customers and they keep coming back for more."

Instead of listing a "five-page website," we might say: "Create a five-page website that speaks to your [ideal client], so that prospects immediately understand what you offer and book a call with you."

While the connection between our ideas and their goals might seem obvious to us, it's not always obvious to them. We must make sure they see it too. "So that" statements connect the idea you're suggesting to the outcome they want. And the more you use them throughout your brief, the clearer it will be that working with you will help them achieve their goals.

Remember, we don't want to give our clients more work to do. We want to do the work *for them* and give them the experience that working with us makes their lives easier. "So that" statements help make those connections.

That's a high-level description of the critical sections of a successful brief. And while it's important you make it your own and specific to your industry and clientele, I urge you to pause before adding additional sections. Consider whether you're adding them to beef up the brief because you think it needs it to justify your prices, or if those extra sections are actually adding value.

Let's go through some of the biggest mistakes I see people make when writing an LP brief so you can avoid them.

Mistake #1: Making It Too Long

If you're an overachiever like so many people in my world, you're going to think the more information you give, the more valuable it will feel.

You may also find yourself questioning whether you have enough value to offer. Ironically, this often gets worse the more experienced you get. It's called the Dunning-Kruger effect: when you're just starting out, a little knowledge makes you feel like an expert. But the more you actually know, the more you realize how complex everything is—and the less confident you feel. The result is knowing more while feeling less certain. That discomfort often leads experts to overload LP briefs with too much information because they're worried about not providing enough value.

Sometimes this comes from being long-winded and not taking the time to edit. As my favorite saying goes: "If I had more time, I would have written a shorter letter." When you have valuable information to share, it can take more time, not less, to cull it down into a concise brief.

Regardless of the reason, it's a mistake to make the brief even a sentence longer than it needs to be. Part of what we're trying to convey is that solving this problem will be *easy* for them. Will it feel easy if they have to read through 20+ pages? Even if the info is good, that's a lot to digest. I've seen extra-long briefs that are twice as long as they need to be because they include entire pages of generic, educational information explaining the service. Rather than use your brief to teach your client about finance, law, architecture, or marketing, use the recommendations section to share only strategies explicitly relevant to them and explain how. If you need to first teach someone about brand messaging, it means your recommendation about their brand message isn't making a strong case on its own.

When I first taught this process to Ilana Preuss from Recast City back in 2020, she took to it immediately. Recast City helps local economies thrive by bringing back small-scale manufacturing. At the time, Ilana was still doing one-on-one work, helping local governments invest in revitalizing their towns and cities.

She had an enormous amount of valuable insight to offer city planners and was deeply committed to helping them succeed. When she learned how to sell her advice through the Lead Product Brief, she went all in. She had no trouble selling the LP, which was priced under $1,000, yet after upselling a few early clients, things stalled. Clients thanked her, told her how valuable the brief was, and said they needed time to digest everything. They promised to come back later.

When I reviewed the briefs she was delivering, the issue was immediately clear. They were essentially research papers—dense, long, and packed with excellent advice, but not actually serving the client as intended. It paralyzed prospects to receive so much important information. It gave them the illusion they could read, reread, and figure things out on their own before hiring Ilana.

Of course, we both know what usually happens with a dense pile of information that requires action. Not much.

I told her to cut the briefs down by at least half. Keep the key recommendations. Remove the rest. Make the big picture obvious and take out anything that made it feel like a handbook.

She followed the advice, and almost immediately clients began closing from the LP. The following year, she closed so many that she brought in over $100,000 in January alone. More importantly, those clients actually hired her to implement the work and got the results they needed.

Mistake #2: Being Too Generic

"You need a clear brand message and a consistent visual brand across all touchpoints."

"You need a plan for paying down your credit card debt."

"You need to deal with the issues that are keeping you stuck."

These are not valuable recommendations—they're surface-level suggestions you could frankly make to someone without doing an interview. They're more along the lines of what you might recommend in a proposal, not an LP brief.

The value and power of the LP brief is that you're taking what could be generic advice for anyone and making it relevant.

"Your brand message *should be...* Your visual brand *should look like...*"

"Here are the three steps you should take based on your current debt situation to pay it down..."

"You are stuck because of XYZ and here's a plan to help you

get unstuck."

Then elaborate on the specifics. Give them answers here, not advice to get answers. If they need a clear brand message, give them an idea of what kind of brand message would be right for them. You don't need to have this finalized, but you do need a clear and specific direction. Explain in great detail what visuals you're recommending—black and white moody photography of landscapes, or bright and playful primary colors and textures layered to feel tactile. These descriptions paint very different pictures.

In a financial advice context, this might look like clearly outlining how much money should be allocated each month to each credit card and on what timeline. In a coaching context, it could mean explaining the exercises you use to surface and release limiting beliefs and naming the exact beliefs you've already identified for the client during your interview.

An easy way to test whether you're doing this well: read through your brief and ask yourself, "If I change the name on the brief to give these recommendations to a different client, would they still make sense?" If yes, you haven't made it specific enough to this client.

Note you'll likely give similar advice to all your clients, especially if you own a clear niche. Part of the reason you're able to develop expertise is by seeing the same challenges over and over again and having a solution that works and has worked for many others. Even if the general advice is the same for all clients, the specifics to that client is what makes this brief so valuable.

Mistake #3: Giving Advice You Can't Help With
When you know a lot about your clients and their needs, you'll likely have advice outside your area of expertise. You might be a career coach who helps people redo their resume and tap into their network to find their next move, so you've naturally developed ideas about their LinkedIn profile—even though you don't actually help them with it. Let's say you think their LinkedIn bio needs upgrading for them to be successful. You have three options:
1. Give your suggested edits in your LP brief and either include it in your package or do the work anyway as a surprise. Use this project as an excuse to get better at writing LinkedIn bios so you can include it as a service in the future.
2. Give your suggested edits in your LP brief and recommend someone they can hire for a flat fee to help them (ideally, you already know who and what their fee is).
3. Don't suggest updating their LinkedIn bio in the LP brief if you're not going to help them.

In this example, I'd recommend option one because it addresses the real need, not just the requested one. While it requires more time upfront, developing that skill pays off because future clients are likely to need the same thing.

In other situations, it may not be a skill worth building. For example, let's say you're designing someone's brand and website and you think they should start a YouTube channel. This might be a good strategy, yet it's a huge undertaking. If you're not offering to do this as part of your project and you don't want to offer it as a service, decide how critical it is. If mission-critical, bring in a partner to deliver this and include them in your proposal, or suggest they work with them after they work with you. Or decide that although YouTube marketing is a good idea, it's outside the scope of the project right now and keep it out of your brief completely. You weren't hired to develop a marketing plan, and telling someone to "make a YouTube channel" is a big, unwieldy recommendation.

The intended effect of these extra recommendations is that the client gets a full plan. The actual effect is usually overwhelm, which leads to inaction—especially if you can't help them with it. This leaves them trying to figure out how much time and money it will take. They may go off looking for someone to hire, and that person makes a really good case for why they should start with their YouTube channel instead of their website or brand because it can take time to get off the ground and it's where they can get clients directly. If this happens, your recommendation has sent your client off to work with someone else instead of you, when they really *do* need their brand and website sorted out first.

Your Moving Forward section at the end should be a project consisting only of deliverables you mentioned or described in the recommendations section. This way, after they read and agree with your recommendations, the proposal at the end feels like a neat and tidy box that makes the vision feel attainable if they hire only you.

Advice to Make Your Lead Product Brief Upsell

Connect to Results

Make sure you connect your advice to the results and outcome the client wants. Do this at the beginning, throughout, and *definitely* at the end. Because even though someone might hire an architect to help build a house, what they *really* want is to build their forever home that feels like it was made for them. Or maybe what they really want is to make a house that has mass appeal because they're building it to sell. Or maybe their goal is to rent it out for a maximum price so they can use the income to achieve financial freedom.

A client who hires you for a new website may say they just want a new website, but what they *really* want is more or better customers. And they don't want more customers just to have more customers—perhaps they want them because that will allow them to franchise their business, which will allow them to support their aging parents and pay for their kids' college.

There's *the thing* you're hired for, and then there's the *big reason* they want it. Always look for that bigger reason and tie your plan to it.

Bring it to Life with Specific References

I alluded to this before but it's really big and bears repeating. Instead of relying on common words to explain your ideas, specific words and references will make your brief much more powerful.

For example, in creative services, if you describe your vision for the design as bold colors, minimalist, and geometric, that's pretty good. But if you take it a step further and reference Matisse block prints versus Southwest Art or Montessori vibes—which are all very different but could all be described as bold colors, minimalist, and geometric—you can see how each of those references instantly makes you picture a completely different look.

These references help stimulate the imagination of your clients and more clearly convey what you're suggesting. When they can picture it in their minds and they love it, they'll be so excited that you get them and that you have this clear idea of where their brand needs to go. Again, this is why they'll see you as the only option to help them.

This can apply to any industry. If you're in the financial world and you're talking to a client about their financial goals, it's the difference between saying "extra money for vacations" and "extra money so you can spend your summer in Paris and your Christmas holiday skiing in the Alps and still not stress that your mortgage will get paid."

Sell Your Ideas
There was this big "don't drink and drive" ad campaign in the 1990s. Millions of dollars spent; it was ubiquitous. You would think that something as obvious as "don't risk your life unnecessarily" would be an easy message to convey, yet surprisingly, it required a lot of advertising and marketing to sell that idea to everyone.

Similarly, even if you're giving your clients a brilliant strategy, that doesn't mean you can be lazy about how you present it. Don't say, "You should think about adding a little more personality to your website copy." Instead, sell it: "You are a badass through and through, and your copy needs to show you off with the energy and enthusiasm that you bring to every conversation." One just gives advice, and the other hypes the reader and inspires them.

Write with Conviction and Authority
I cringe at jargon and find that when people try to sound professional, they end up sounding flat, boring, and like unintelligent talking heads (I said what I said!). Instead of speaking passively to sound professional, use the active voice to speak directly to the client with authority in a way that excites them.

Passive voice is that wishy-washy way of writing where the subject gets buried—like "this brand would benefit from a more interesting homepage photo." Active voice flips that: the subject does the action, clear and direct, like "you need disruptive photography right on the homepage that grabs the attention of the exact people you want to work with and insists that they scroll down to learn more." It conveys confidence and pulls readers in with energy. They feel your authority, not some detached expert droning on. Passive is less powerful and harder to get excited about. Active owns it, excites them, and makes them trust that you're the one leading the charge.

If your brief isn't getting your client excited about the possibilities, then it really isn't reaching its full potential.

You are their cheerleader. Act like it.

Shift in Thinking: Lead from the First Step

The Lead Product isn't just a way to sell more easily—it's a way to gain control over your sales.

When you have one clear entry point, one defined way people start working with you, everything simplifies: how you talk about your work, how others think of you and refer clients to you, how you close clients, and how clients perceive your value. Instead of juggling multiple offers or customizing every conversation, you're selling *one* thing that leads to everything else. And when you have that clarity and simplicity, you have more options.

Rebecca McCarthy is a great example of what this looks like in practice. She runs a one-person career coaching business, helping clients land their next role through resumes, interview prep, and personal branding. When she simplified her process and led with a paid Lead Product, she was able to raise her prices and make her business far easier to run. Sales became easier, clients were better qualified, and she started reliably generating $10,000 months without overworking—which was her goal.

But what mattered more than the money was the confidence this gave her over her sales. When Rebecca decided to step back from her business to spend more time with her teenage son before a major life milestone, she was able to do it intentionally and without fear. She knew exactly how to generate new business and felt confident closing clients into her packages, which meant she could step away—and turn it back on—when she was ready.

That's the real power of a simple, repeatable system that's easy to run: it gives you the ability to choose how and when you work.

No matter what industry you're in, a paid Lead Product will change how you show up, how you sell, how clients perceive your value, and how naturally you upsell into higher-priced work. I've seen people adapt the strategy in different ways—using live presentations, recorded videos, or workshops—but for me, a simple written document with no bells and whistles has been incredibly effective. I've sold LPs priced from $650 to $10,000, and upsold them into $30,000–$100,000 projects.

While I encourage you to make the format your own, it's important to stick to the core framework and principles. What I've outlined here are the essential building blocks of an LP that actually converts, based on thousands of real examples from my own business and from clients and students who've implemented it successfully.

And the impact doesn't stop at the sale. The Lead Product sets the tone for the entire working relationship. When trust is built upfront and clients are already looking to you to lead, the larger project becomes easier to guide. The LP creates the confidence and momentum needed to run high-level projects—especially Intensives—with far less friction and more valuable outcomes.

I'll show you how in the next chapter!

Take Action:

1. **How many hours did you waste last month writing free proposals for people who never hired you?** Add it up and multiply it by the minimum hourly rate you would charge. That's how much unpaid work you're doing while wondering why you're not making enough money.
2. **What story are you telling yourself about why you can't charge for discovery work?** That prospects won't pay? That it's not how things are done? That you're not established enough yet? Write it down. Then ask: is that story making you money—or keeping you stuck?
3. **When you give away strategic advice for free, are you being generous—or are you being scared?** Be honest. Are you "adding value" or are you hoping if you give enough away, they'll finally see you're worth hiring? One builds trust. The other builds resentment.

If You Only Take One Thing From This Chapter:

Free proposals position you as an order-taker, not an expert. When you charge for the first step—the Lead Product—you build trust before the sale, qualify serious clients, and upsell into bigger projects without the desperation dance. Stop giving away your best thinking for free and wondering why clients don't value it. Charge for it and they will value it! That's how experts operate.

Get more info on how to deliver the Lead Product for your business: scalesolobook.com/resources

PART 3: NO BS SALES

PART FOUR

No BS Delivery

I remember Steve saying to me once, frustrated in the middle of another never-ending project, "Imagine if I could just make a client their brand and website and just hand it to them. No revisions. No meetings. I make it, they buy it. Can we make a business like that? Wouldn't that be the dream?"

Steve is a creative. An artist. He wants to use his talents to make great work.

He does *not* want to go back and forth with a client ten times, tweaking a pixel here or a word there, until they think it is perfect. He already thought it was perfect. That is why he sent it.

And whether you create visuals, systems, strategies, or something else entirely, it is deeply appealing when a client gets out of your way, lets you do your best work, and then thanks you for it without edits.

When you are truly an expert, the quality of the work you

deliver is extremely important to you. Sometimes, it's more important than being *liked* by your client, though you want that too. If you have ever had to water down or butcher your work to please a client and walked away feeling frustrated and a little gross, you know exactly what I mean. That desire to do your best work can sometimes clash with the desire to be liked.

Back in 2013, when Steve was talking about this, having clients say *yes* to all our work, without edits, was the dream—yet our reality looked nothing like that.

When we were operating under the default model, most of our projects ran past their intended timelines. No matter how carefully I mapped out phases and deadlines, something always seemed to derail the plan.

My timelines were designed by weeks. Week 1: moodboard. Week 2: logo. And so forth.

That meant the timeline was fluid and was treated as such. I would email work out, and then wait for feedback and approval. But I rarely knew *when* I would hear back. When I did, I never knew whether it would be approved, if there would be requests for changes, or how many rounds of changes the client would request. And how long would those changes take to get approved?

I was at the mercy of the client's schedule, and how high on their priority list I was (usually not that high). Every time we got the ball back in our court, we moved quickly. We were incentivized to move quickly because our next payments were tied to completing project milestones. The client, on the other hand, had little incentive to respond to any timeline.

We were playing hot potato, except the client had oven mitts on, and we did not.

Whenever we got pulled into a project that seemed to stretch on endlessly, Steve and I would openly question how ridiculous the whole thing had become. Clients were paying for design, but the bulk of our time was swallowed by scheduling chaos, long email threads, minor tweaks, and punch lists—far more effort than the work itself ever required.

I remember when Steve shared this wish with me, and we entertained the idea of making brands and logos and putting them up on an online shop for people to buy.

"Get our amazing brands for a fraction of the price—just buy them off the shelf!"

This fantasy would allow us to have everything we wanted, without any of the frustrating downside: we could spend all our time doing the *creative* work we loved best, get rid of all the bullshit project management—meetings, phone calls, and chasing, all of which stressed me out—and get paid in full for our work.

Eventually, of course, we realized our $3,000 1-Day Brandup was actually much more profitable than even our big $30,000 projects. At first, our Brandups functioned like VIP days—we were essentially hired for a day of focused work. I told the clients upfront that they would get as much as we could design in one day. We were clear with clients that we'd design as much as possible in that time, and that the faster they made decisions and approved work, the more they'd get out of the day.

We set expectations somewhere in the middle—a logo and a homepage—but most clients got much more. That promise of extra deliverables meant that most of our first clients had no changes to any of the work because they all wanted as much as they could get, which was usually additional pages and collateral like business cards.

But when we started offering Brandups to prospects who had originally received a proposal for a $30,000 full branding project, which was much more than we could deliver in a 1-day VIP-style engagement, we began to shift how we saw it. Yes, they would still get as much as we could give them in the time-frame, but these were more robust projects, and we didn't want to give them less than they needed.

Our first Brandup with this new thinking was a 2-day Brandup for $5,000 for Stash Wealth, where we rebranded the design and built a simple but full website.

We had already pitched them our $30,000 brand and website package months before, and they wanted it, but it was a hefty price tag for a new business. When I went back to them and told them we could deliver the same project but for $5,000 *if* they were willing to basically trust us (i.e., not push back on the design) and make decisions on the spot, they gave us an emphatic *yes*.

I knew I wasn't going to feel comfortable ending the Brandup on day two without completely finishing it. We needed to complete the whole project, and I wanted it to be amazing and our best work. I wanted to do right by our clients, and this was going to be one of our first case studies to show off for future work. So it couldn't really be an abbreviated version of the big project we originally pitched; it needed to be our *best* work to prove the model, just delivered in two days instead of four months.

We couldn't leave it to chance.

Steve had always done some prep work beforehand for our VIP days, but those VIP days were meant to be only a day of work. For this Brandup, we prepared more heavily. I wrote all the website copy ahead of time, and Steve followed his full process, as he would for any "normal" client: designing a couple of logo options, the website homepage, and even making some fun custom icons. By the time the clients came in, we had done as much as we felt we could without their feedback. We didn't make any interior pages or collateral because we wanted to get approval first. We figured we would incrementally show them the work and show them more as they approved it.

Since they came in ready to approve things, the first morning went really smoothly. We made a few tweaks to the final logo right there on the spot, they approved it, and we moved on. We showed them the top of the homepage with the main tagline I had written, and they loved it, so we continued on with the rest of the homepage. They gave some feedback, Steve made some edits—approved. After that, Steve got to work on the interior pages while I went through the rest of the website copy, took feedback, and made edits. By the end of the first day, Steve had the approved copy on the website and showed them a few interior pages.

Since we had gotten through so much on day one, I told them to come in after lunch on day two so we could have some concentrated time to execute a bunch of collateral. I assigned them to draft a couple of blog posts we could use. Editing blog posts hadn't been included in the original LP brief because I hadn't suggested it, but when it came up on day one, I realized they really needed one, and we added it since things were going so well. By the time they arrived on day two, we had the website almost completely done, business cards, and all the identity materials they needed (envelopes, letterhead—wow paper goods, this sounds like a lifetime ago!).

And because everything matched the brand they approved the day before, there wasn't much feedback. I spent the second afternoon suggesting improvements for their blog posts while Steve wrapped up the website, checked the links, saved out all the final logo files, and purchased the stock photos and fonts. We couldn't make their website live that day because their compliance department needed to okay it, but they did send it off while we were there.

By 6pm on day two, they were amazed that the entire project was done.

And we were so excited that we just proved we could do a full branding and website project with the client in only two days by eliminating **all the BS.**

The Chaos in Your Delivery

Everything in your process right now that isn't directly adding value to your client's desired outcome is BS to eliminate.

Sometimes it can be hard to see because we are so used to doing things the way everyone does them. So let's start with the obvious BS:
- Scheduling and rescheduling meetings
- Following up on previous communications that have gone unanswered

- Chasing clients for information, feedback, or materials you need to move the project forward
- Rearranging your schedule, because the hours you set aside for a project need to shift in response to moving client deadlines or changes in their feedback schedule
- Imagining all the worst-case scenarios when a client doesn't pay an invoice immediately, doesn't respond quickly to work sent, or doesn't respond to emails in a timely manner
- Unnecessary meetings (while some meetings are necessary for a successful project, I promise you're having more of them than you need to)

You'll notice quite a bit of this BS is magnified by clients not responding. This is not because your clients suck; it's just the world we live in. We're all juggling a million inputs, and even with good intentions, messages get missed or forgotten.

How many times have you opened your email, social media, or a platform you belong to just to grab one piece of information, only to get pulled into everything else there? A few minutes later, you realize you're distracted, close the tab to get back to work, and immediately remember the thing you went there to find in the first place.

I'm embarrassed to say I have gone through this loop two or even three times before actually getting the info that I need.

Talk about BS!

Even the most disciplined person usually has quite a few things fighting for their attention at any given time, especially the kind of successful clients you want to work with.

And as important as this project might be to them, it's probably not *as* important as a few other things on their plate—professional and personal. So it's no wonder that simply getting things from your clients promptly is a challenge that is filling up your time unnecessarily.

We'll talk about how to handle that in a bit, but first, let's talk about BS that is not always so obvious.

Revisions

Depending on the type of work you do, client revisions can either be a crucial part of achieving the best outcome or they can actively pull the project off track. Productive revisions clarify, refine, and strengthen the work. Unproductive ones introduce noise.

For example, when we rebranded *EthicsMatters LLC*, the consultancy and training company founded by Luann Van Campen, client reviews were not just helpful; they were necessary. While I could confidently shape the overall messaging, positioning, and brand voice, Luann needed to carefully review and correct or refine the highly technical and nuanced biopharmaceutical bioethics language. That kind of revision didn't dilute the work—it ensured accuracy in areas that were outside my expertise.

Revisions that water down the work or take it in the wrong direction are usually driven by personal taste or impulse and are BS to be eliminated—like when a client once saw a logo they liked with a metal sheen, and suddenly wanted to see their logo with a metal sheen, even though it made absolutely no sense with their brand.

Scope Creep

When items or time get added to a project without payment, it doesn't just add to the time you will spend on the project itself. It adds additional BS to your mind and schedule as you have to rearrange your schedule and communicate more to accommodate. There is untrackable energy and time spent without any additional compensation, and it needs to go.

It usually shows up as the classic "can we just add this one small thing?" request—except the thing is never actually small. Or when the work has already been approved, but then a friend, sister, or cousin with some background in your field weighs in, and suddenly there's a request for "just a quick adjustment."

Clients use the word *just* because they're trying to communicate that they don't think it's a big deal and won't require a meaningful amount of your time. But anyone who has ever agreed to a "just" request knows the truth: it takes longer than the client thinks, longer than you think, and it almost always opens the door to more changes that weren't part of the original scope.

Change Requests

Anytime a client needs to change a project scope, either by changing it or adding something, even if they are going to compensate you for it, it can end up being BS if the additional compensation doesn't account for the time and energy spent making the change.

And you might be thinking *that's just part of the job, and besides, if they're willing to pay for add-ons, why not welcome the extra work? What's wrong with that?*

There's nothing wrong with it. But it's inefficient, and hard to make profitable. And what I'd like to show you is that *most* of this BS can be eliminated… by intensifying your process.

The Intensive

The **Intensives Model** is what stopped us from working for months just to end up broke and exhausted—and started running projects that ended in two days, at 6:00 p.m. sharp, with clients thrilled, satisfied, and singing our praises.

Instead of chasing client approval through endless rounds of feedback, we created a process that gets clients *on board and excited* about the work we've already done—so that by the time they see it, all that's left are a few tweaks to finalize the work.

Now, instead of dragging out projects for months until clients are "happy," we sell **$30,000–60,000 Brandup Intensives** that take place in 48 hours. And because of this model, we spend *90% of our time actually doing the work*—our favorite work—the kind that gets our best results, not the watered-down version we used to end up with after weeks of compromises and changes.

The Intensives Model is not a faster version of the old way of doing things. It's not a "VIP day" or "day rate" approach either. Those are still time-for-money models—and there's a hard cap on what you can charge for them.

Intensives are something else entirely: a **completely dif-**

ferent way of working with clients that eliminates the very problems that keep you unprofitable.

Our Intensive is a 1-3 day session with clients to deliver and finalize an entire custom brand and website. The days themselves are designed to bring the client on board, get them excited, committed, and enthusiastic, and finalize the project so it is launched and finished at the end of the final day.

For other businesses, the structure of an Intensive can vary. It might be a few Intensives spread out over a week or two. It might even be a few Intensives that deliver phases of the project, with a month or months in between. It can even be applied to the retainer model so that you have monthly or quarterly Intensives to deliver ongoing work.

The purpose of the Intensive is not to do it faster; it's to do it more intensively to shorten the timeline. The quality of the output should be the same or better than what you would do in a traditional process.

But the time you spend on it will shrink because you will eliminate some, if not all, of the BS.

What Makes Intensives Different

Intensives start with **value-based package pricing**, not deliverables. We don't just promise a list of deliverables; we connect the package to the result, and what the client will ultimately achieve because of it. The first step is always the **Lead Product**, which defines what success actually looks like for the client. The Intensive execution of that plan in the shortest timeline possible to maximize efficiency and results.

We're able to do this because of the clarity everyone has on the project, process, and goals from day one. The brief becomes the north star. Personal opinions and last-minute changes don't derail anything because the project is already on a bullet train with a clearly defined schedule and the destination in sight.

For our Intensives, there's only one deadline for the client: the date they must submit everything we need for the project. No delays waiting on client inputs; if the client doesn't meet their deadline, the project gets rescheduled.

That clarity alone eliminates much of the frustration businesses face.

We also find that Intensives benefit from higher energy and enthusiasm. There's usually a lot of enthusiasm from both sides when you kick off a project. But then it drags on for months and months, and that enthusiasm wanes. Imagine if the energy you both have on that first call was sustained throughout the project.

Intensives get to ride the wave of enthusiasm from start to finish—and the client feels just as energized at the end as they did at the start.

Because the process is so streamlined, we can do focused work with one client at a time—and then when it's over, it's *over.* There are no dangling tasks, no open loops, no "quick little updates."

If the client wants more, that's a new offer.

I've honed this process over years in my business and in hundreds of others. While not everyone will have an Intensive as intense as two days, it is absolutely doable—even when the project requires multiple deadlines and multiple stakeholders. We can *always* apply this principle, whatever the business, to trim away the BS that eats up time, energy, and profit.

Sara Chambers, the strategic brain behind *Elly & Nora* Creative, is a great example of intensifying a process that still requires many moving parts. She's technically a solo business owner—no full-time employees—but she's never been the one to execute client deliverables. From day one, her role has been owner, strategist, and creative director. She leads the thinking, sets the direction, manages the project, and coordinates a team of contractors who handle design and the website builds. On paper, this looks like many traditional agencies. In reality, it's often where things collapse: too many moving parts, fuzzy scope, endless revisions, bloated timelines, and thin margins. Sara applied the No BS Model to this structure, transforming it into a business that is both highly profitable and surprisingly calm.

The first big shift came from fully integrating the Lead Product, which fundamentally changed how Sara positioned herself and how projects began. She describes a noticeable difference in client relationships, noting that the LP establishes authority and trust before executing.

Since she works with larger clients and more complex brands, the LP is followed by a deeper strategy Intensive—an in-depth working session where the full strategic foundation is locked in. By the time execution begins, there is no ambiguity about direction, priorities, or success.

The other major shift was how Sara scheduled her projects. Because she is the creative director and strategist, her personal work is intentionally front-loaded: nearly all of her hands-on client work happens in the first two weeks, focused on strategy and copy. After that, contractors handle all execution while she shifts into coordination and light oversight. To intensify the work, Sara schedules only two projects per month and books each new client into the next available slot. So even when larger projects take two to three months overall, she is rarely in constant client mode. She meets with clients to present work, yet by that time her heavy lift is complete, and her team handles the rest. Because the process is so tight and expectations are set early, she experiences virtually no pushback, revisions, or scope creep. She says it's night and day from how she used to run the work, where similar projects would have taken six months or longer and involved much more back-and-forth. The result is a business where Sara can take on large, complex projects, stay in control of her time, and scale profit without chaos—proof that Intensives aren't about speed alone, but about scheduling work in a way that protects both your margins and your sanity.

One reason Intensives can help you be so efficient (and free!) is because of something I call **Chunk and Stack.**

The Chunk and Stack™ Method

Research from the American Psychological Association shows that completing a project from start to finish without switching to others is far more efficient than juggling multiple projects at once. Chances are you've heard the claim that there's really no such thing as multi-tasking—that it takes our brains time to shift mental gears. In fact, task-switching can reduce productivity by up to 40%. For someone working 40 hours a week, that's up to 16 hours of lost time due to inefficiency alone. Can you imagine what you could do with an extra 16 hours a week?!

This is why I am a firm believer in the **Chunk and Stack Method™**—both for client projects, and for how you manage your schedule.

The idea is simple: schedule projects consecutively, not concurrently. Instead of working on multiple clients at a time over long periods, where you are switching between projects daily, you chunk your projects so you only work on one at a time. Then you stack those projects, so you work on a project to completion before starting the next.

Imagine this: let's say it takes Steve 40 hours *total* to do the creative work for a project, not including any of the BS, just executing the project for four hours every week for ten weeks.

Now let's imagine that he instead decided to work full-time on that project for one week, eight hours a day for five days, which also equals 40 hours.

If we apply the research above by focusing on a single client and project and doing nothing else, he gets the productivity benefit of that focused, concentrated time. Instead of the 40 hours it would have taken him over the course of weeks, he does it in 40% less time, and it now takes him only 24 hours, or three eight-hour days of work.

Since that's the best-case scenario, let's meet in the middle and pretend he only received a 20% benefit in efficiency. That same project takes him 32 hours instead of 40 hours, or four eight-hour days. That's still a full day freed up.

And that's just the beginning. There are many additional benefits to doing this project in four consecutive days rather than spreading it out over ten weeks.

First, our hypothetical scenario is just for Steve doing the creative work. It doesn't account for all the BS of meetings, chasing clients, and scope creep. The great thing about doing a project in a concentrated timeline is that you can almost completely eliminate these things just by chunking the project.

When you deliver a project to a client over a couple of days, these days are scheduled and a top priority for them. Rather than being one of many things on that client's to-do list, you are on their calendar. I don't know about you, but if I have something that absolutely *must* get done, I put it on my *calendar*, not my to-do list.

When we are a priority on our client's calendar, we are no longer at the whim of all the things they might be juggling. They know this is when the project is happening and finishing, and so it becomes a non-negotiable part of their schedule.

There also isn't time in between meetings for a project to change scope or direction. If you work with a business for months, you are at the whim of whatever changes might be going on. I've seen projects that lasted so long that by the time they were wrapping up, the client had decided to expand, which they should have factored into the website. But these kinds of big changes rarely happen over a few days.

And the best part of Chunk and Stack for a small-business owner like you? You get control over your schedule back.

Chunk and Stack means you can schedule clients back-to-back, or schedule weeks in between. When you are only running Intensives like we did, the time in between Intensives is yours, full stop.

In May of 2017, we chunked and stacked five $20,000 projects in a row, banked $100,000, and then went to Europe for seven weeks with absolutely no clients to alert or respond to. We were able to check out completely, and come home to projects booked on our calendar starting a month after our return.

One reason I've heard people bristle at this idea is that they say they *just* want a steady income. They prefer a project spread over months because they like the idea of collecting $5,000 each month for six months.

I will talk about this more in the next chapter, but here's how it relates to Chunk and Stack: If you can get paid $30,000 upfront to start and finish a project, the only reason you would logically be better off spreading those payments out over six months would be because you can't trust yourself *not* spend the money.

It's just a psychological money game we play with ourselves.

I hope you can see why, financially, they are the same ($30,000 upfront is actually even more money if you can put it in a high-yield savings account at 4%, you can actually generate an extra $600 from it over six months. But you definitely won't make *less.*)

On the other hand, you *could* make less with a six-month payment plan. $30,000 upfront is less risky because it's guaranteed. Sure, the client said they would pay you $5,000/month for six months. Sure, they signed a contract. Yes, they are nice people, and you have a good relationship with them…. but I've seen it *all*. If someone's business goes under, or they get into trouble and have to push the project off (until later or indefinitely), or something totally unrelated happens in their personal life, that money is just not guaranteed. You will always be in a more financially secure position if you work on shorter timelines and collect the fee upfront rather than spreading it out over time.

So if it's logically better to collect upfront rather than spread our payment out over months, all we have to work on is how it *feels*. (I'll talk about how in the next chapter!)

Hopefully you are sufficiently sold on the idea of intensifying your projects! Now let's talk about *how* to make it work.

The Intensive - 3 Things You Need to be Successful

Intensifying your projects is as much about tactical changes in your process as it is about psychological changes in how you show up for your clients. So before we tackle the *how*, let's talk about the even more important part of *who* you need to become for this to work like a charm.

ONE: The Trust Bank

I started to understand why the Intensives worked so well for us on a random Tuesday night in mid-2015 at, of all places, Walgreens.

Steve and I were waiting for a prescription, doing what we did in those early days—running every little errand together. He picked up a book from the wire rack, one of those cheap paperbacks that scream "self-help" in shiny embossed letters, and started thumbing through it, more out of boredom than interest, until a phrase caught his eye.

"Listen to this," he said. "It's talking about something called a 'Love Bank' and how every relationship has one."

The concept was simple: in every relationship—romantic or not—you're constantly making deposits and withdrawals. A deposit is anything that builds trust or affection: showing up when you said you would, keeping your word, or surprising someone with a thoughtful gesture. A withdrawal is the opposite: breaking a promise, missing a deadline, letting someone down.

And here's the kicker—the book explained that one withdrawal isn't equal to one deposit. Withdrawals are unfortunately weighted much more heavily; a single one can wipe out dozens of deposits.

I could immediately see this dynamic in play throughout my entire life <scream face>.

We didn't buy the book, but the idea stuck. We kept talking about it long after Walgreens, because it felt so true not just for us, but for our business.

That's when I realized every client relationship also has a Love Bank. Only in business, I call it the Trust Bank.

Think about it. We're making deposits to our clients at every single step of the process, assuming we're doing what we say we're going to do. When you tell a client, "I'll send that over on Friday at 12pm," and then you do, you've just made a little deposit. They ask you a question, you say you'll find the answer and get back to them today, then you do, and another deposit. Every time you deliver work as promised you are making deposits.

But when you drop the ball? Even on something small?

That's a withdrawal. And withdrawals count more heavily than deposits.

I once had a student who nailed her Lead Product interview. She did the work. She created a thoughtful, strategic brief. The client was impressed. But on the cover page, she had accidentally misspelled the client's business name. One small, but important, typo. And the client was furious.

Was it fair? Maybe not. But it illustrates how, even though she had done such great work up until that point, there weren't enough deposits in the Trust Bank at that time to counterbalance the weight of that small but not insignificant withdrawal. The client interpreted it as a broader lack of attention to detail and, without enough experience to know otherwise, decided not to hire her.

Withdrawals are not just egregious mistakes or blatantly poor customer service—obviously, if you miss deadlines and do poor, shoddy work, you'll accumulate a mountain of Trust Bank Debt. But there are other withdrawals you might be making that you aren't even aware of.

Here are some subtle ways you can turn minor withdrawals into powerful deposits.

When you're doing a perfectly fine job, but not intentionally minding your Trust Bank, it can look like saying you'll get them the invoice and contract to kick off the project, but not giving them a time and date for when you'll send it. And then sending it the following day, in the afternoon.

It can look like telling a client you are going to send them a piece of work on Tuesday, then sending it at 10pm on Tuesday.

It's answering emails at night and on the weekends, giving

clients work earlier than you said you would, and saying "yes" when they ask you to add something to the project out of scope without even discussing it.

Even though you might think that last part is going above and beyond for a client, these things aren't adding to your Trust Bank, and can actually deplete it. I get it. I've been guilty of all these things, too. And then I learned what building your Trust Bank with intention looks like.

When a client says they want to move forward, you give clear and specific instructions.

"Great, I'm excited to get started. As soon as we get off this call, I will send you the contract and invoice, and I will need that back by the end of the day tomorrow to solidify the dates we chose." And then you send the email within 30 minutes.

Minding your Trust Bank means that when you say, "I will send you the work Tuesday," you then send it at 8am Tuesday, so it is sitting in their inbox when they start working.

Importantly, it also means holding boundaries around communication times and project scope. It might feel like answering emails quickly, even if it's after work hours or on the weekend, is just great customer service. You might assume adding more work is overdelivering and therefore always valuable. But what it really does is blur the lines around expectations. And because you've blurred the lines, you will risk losing trust when you inadvertently don't deliver at that level, which the client has now come to expect.

When boundaries and expectations aren't clearly defined, the client will fill in the blanks for you. And when they do, you won't know what they are, and then you'll be frustrated when they seem to start asking for more than you think is appropriate.

I used to pride myself on replying to emails immediately (and I was a stressball, always refreshing my inbox so I *could* respond right away), but all this does is train your client to expect immediate responses—day or night, and on weekends. And since it's not possible to be on top of your email *all* the time (even if you are tied to your phone 18 hours a day) you simply cannot meet that expectation that *you* are setting.

By holding boundaries and creating and maintaining consistent expectations, you ensure you'll always meet your clients' expectations, which builds trust. And while none of the examples above are going to make or break a relationship, they do subtly erode the potency of your word.

What's even more important is how much more value these boundaries can *add* to the engagement.

When I was just a couple of years into my business, I worked with my first business coach. I met her through BNI networking, and I liked her a lot; she was spunky, enthusiastic, and very encouraging. And she was incredibly generous with her time.

Our arrangement: $500 a month for bi-monthly two-hour meetings, plus email support as needed.

We usually met at a place like Astro, one of those classic old-school Greek diners in midtown, because they don't rush you to leave. We needed that because these meetings would often run much longer than two hours. If she didn't have a meeting right after, she was happy to keep talking to me for a third or even fourth hour. Sounds like a lot of over-delivery, right? I know that was her intention. She was very generous, and she really wanted to help me, so she was willing to spend as much time as she could with me.

However, I distinctly remember a few times when I had to kind of pull myself away from these meetings because I had other things to do!

Let's compare that to my next business coach, Evan Horowitz. I hired Evan for $1,000 a month, which felt like a lot of money for the four one-hour sessions I was going to get.

But this was set up totally differently. We didn't have any communication outside of those four sessions, aside from social and networking. It's not that he told me I *couldn't* contact him outside of our meetings; he simply didn't offer it.

Our virtual sessions lasted an hour, to the minute. The same way that when you're in a therapy session, at the end of the hour, the therapist says, "Okay, we need to stop now." That was meeting with Evan.

And here's what happened: I would come to those meetings super prepared. I would show up ready to go over the list of things I needed to tackle from our previous meeting, and discuss what I did and didn't accomplish. Then we would spend the hour working, and by the end, we would get clear on my next four or five steps, and that would be it.

I valued Evan's time and our work together so much more. I showed up differently. I prepared ahead of time. I was clear and concise in my communication with him because we only had that hour. I remember him telling me on a few occasions that I was his favorite coachee and best student because I always did *everything* we discussed, which encouraged me even more to make sure I always took the actions I promised. I couldn't let Evan down!

I got so much more out of that relationship because of the **clarity and the boundaries**. And frankly, the fact that our relationship didn't bleed outside of that hour meant that that single hour was worth ten times more than three or four hours with my first business coach.

When you have clear boundaries and when you clearly communicate the value of your time, it's not about withholding or saying no to your client. It's about respecting the value of what you are giving them and the relationship. And your client will get so much more value out of working with you when you do it.

Missing these moments to lead with clarity likely won't tank your relationship. But paying attention to them can turn the value up to an eleven. These subtle but powerful opportunities to build your Trust Bank through deposits will ensure clients' expectations are consistently met and that the project goes smoothly.

This is why I obsess over deposits in the early stages of client relationships.

When I promise a client, "I'll send you the LP on Friday," *my* deadline isn't really Friday. It's Thursday afternoon, so I can schedule the email to go out on Friday at 8am. Because when I say Friday, I want that email in their inbox waiting for them when they sit down at their desk. It's such a simple thing, but it makes a powerful deposit: I said Friday, and they get it first thing Friday. No wondering, no waiting, no anxious refresh of the inbox.

When I get on a call, I start by setting the agenda: "Here's what we're going to cover today…" I end by summarizing: "Here's what we decided, here are your next steps, and here are mine." Then I follow up with a short bullet-point email reiterating the next steps with specific dates.

Each time I do this, it's another reminder that I lead, I deliver, and I keep my word.

These deposits aren't glamorous. They don't require sending expensive client gifts or fancy swag boxes. They're built in the small, unsexy moments: saying what you'll do, and then doing it. Over and over again.

The balance in that Trust Bank determines everything: whether the client hires you, whether they pay your higher price without flinching, whether they follow your lead instead of second-guessing you throughout the process, and whether they rave about you when the project is done. If the work itself is great but the execution and communication are unreliable, that negates the quality of your work. I've been asked for referrals to people I've hired, and I've had to give disclaimers: "They do phenomenal work, but you will have to chase them for answers, and you might not get things when they promise you'll get them…" and most people say, "No thanks, not worth it." Don't let great work be overshadowed by poor processes and follow-through.

If you are uncomfortable with the idea of giving clear and specific dates, times, and instructions because you went into business for freedom, and having to do things so exactly feels like a nightmare, I want you to read something a former student of mine, Executive Coach for entrepreneurs Brandi Holder, shared on LinkedIn:

"One of my coaches, Pia Silva, taught me something years ago that changed how I do things: when you tell your client you're sending something at 3pm, that means 3pm. Not 11am. Not 5pm. Not a day earlier.

On the surface, that's just good customer service.

But I found a deeper meaning. It forces me to run a business free from chaos.

When I commit to something, I must be clear about what's on my plate first. It cuts the fire drills. The last-minute scrambling. The reactive mode that drains everyone.

I used to resist planning because it felt like the opposite of why I went into business for myself. I wanted autonomy. Freedom. Not spreadsheets and timelines.

But planning creates freedom and structure creates space.

When I know what's on my plate, I can make clear commitments. When I make clear commitments, I'm not holding everything in my head. When I'm not holding everything in my head, I have space to think strategically instead of constantly reacting.

Peace in my operations extends naturally to my clients.

That's leadership. Not just knowing what to do but creating the conditions where you can do it without chaos."

She wrote this after receiving the following testimonial from her client:

"*I love how you lay out our expectations and potential roadblocks. It all feels very healthy in its structure and very clear and concise with understanding how this works. A great starting baseline to embark on this. I do much better when I know there's that stuff up ahead."*

The *clarity* is what creates the freedom. It can be scary to give hard deadlines because you're now beholden to them, but it actually takes decision-making off the table. If you are going to send someone a contract right after you get off the call, tell them you're going to do so, and then do it immediately. It will build trust, and is easier than putting it on your to-do list for "later." It sounds so simple, but I know so few of us do it, and it becomes part of the BS that keeps us overwhelmed and spending energy on the wrong things.

The other reason building a Trust Bank is so fundamental to the No BS Model is that you can't lead a client boldly into an Intensive if their Trust Bank isn't full. They're not going to clear their calendar or prioritize you unless they're fully on board with you as the leader. You can't get them to say *yes* to a bold idea on the spot if they don't trust that your word is solid.

A full Trust Bank is critical to the success of an Intensive, and you are the only one who can fill it.

TWO: Captain Your Ship

An Intensive is designed for a client who trusts you, believes you, and *wants* you to lead them to the answer. For an Intensive to go smoothly, clients must arrive ready and excited to follow your lead. If they lack trust, they will go in tentatively, questioningly, and with their guard up. If you've ever had a client question your work, send you ideas or thoughts from someone unrelated to the project, or just tell you they need a lot of time to think about it, *it almost always means there isn't enough trust between you.*

So here's the mindset shift you need to succeed with Intensives: **Clients think they want control—but they don't.**

Imagine boarding a cruise. You unpack, head to the deck, and the captain knocks on your door:

"Welcome aboard! Before we set sail, which way do you want to go?"

You point vaguely toward the sunny horizon, but soon you spot a pretty island and ask her to turn. When you realize the island is surrounded by rocks, you tell her to go back the other way. After hours, you ask when you'll arrive, and the captain shrugs—she doesn't know where you're headed.

That's what happens when clients steer their own projects. You go in circles. Nobody knows where "done" is.

Now imagine a different cruise. The captain greets you and says, "There's an island ahead—the most beautiful one in the world, and I'm going to take you there. Sit back, relax, and enjoy the ride."

You exhale and take a sip of your drink. You trust her to get you there.

That's what it means to be the captain of your ship. And that's exactly the experience we're creating for our clients in an Intensive.

THREE: Be The Guardrails

There is one more mindset shift you need to make if you want to run an effective Intensive: clients want something different from what they say they want. When you ask people what they want, they will usually say more options, more time, and the option to survey for opinions. In practice, I believe the opposite is true. Here's what I mean.

Picture yourself speeding down a highway at 75 miles an hour.

Now imagine that you're approaching a bridge spanning a deep ravine. It's a clear day, the bridge is straight, there's nobody else on it, and it's pretty wide. The drop is hundreds of feet down, but the bridge is obviously very safe.

Now, imagine the bridge has no sides. What do you do? Well, I don't know about you, but I think I would slow the hell down if I were driving 75 mph! In fact, I'd probably crawl across that bridge at ten miles an hour. Thinking about it now even gives me some butterflies.

Okay, but usually bridges have sides. Even moderately high guardrails would suffice to make the bridge feel safe enough that I probably wouldn't even change my speed at all. Without the guardrails there, the threat that you could just run off the side to sudden death feels so much bigger. With the guardrails in place, they provide just enough safety and security to let you keep driving comfortably.

It's very similar to the fear that clients have when we don't provide them with metaphorical sides.

Deep down, clients are scared they made the wrong decision by hiring us. And even when they trust us because of all the deposits that we've made, they're *still* scared that they might make the wrong decisions along the way. When they have hired you to solve a problem at a premium price, the stakes are pretty high; sometimes the fate of their business, and definitely the money they've invested.

So it is very important that they feel they made the *right* choice hiring you.

As experts, we usually focus on doing our best work. Great work is what we owe them most right now.

But to me, great work is a given. What sets us apart from the competition is our ability to make clients feel not just comfortable but *confident in those decisions.*

To confidently lead them and help that confidence land, you need to put guardrails in place throughout the process so they can move forward without fear of falling off along the way.

The moment they feel there's a real risk of making a wrong move that could hurt their business, how do they respond? What does anyone do when they feel threatened?

You tense up, right? You freeze. You slow down. You lose perspective on the big picture and focus on what's going on five feet in front of you.

You start second-guessing yourself, the work, or the person presenting the work.

When we deliver creative work, it's often obvious when fear is driving the feedback. The client likes what they see but still asks for more ideas—not because the work is wrong, but because they're afraid of making the wrong choice. By seeing additional options, they hope to find something that gives them greater certainty, even if what they already have is strong.

Scared clients keep changing their minds because they are second-guessing you, or themselves, or both. They start getting outside opinions, looking for that certainty and safety from others if they aren't getting it from you. They think, "If my wife likes it or my husband likes it, that will make *me* feel better about the decision." So many of the reasons that clients stall projects are that they're afraid to make the wrong move, and they don't even know it.

When they're afraid, they lack the confidence to move swiftly and make decisions.

The success of any Intensive depends on a client feeling comfortable making confident decisions.

So it's our job to create the environment and put up those guardrails. We must create a safe highway for them to speed across the bridge without having to think much about it. We are the guardrails on the side of the road.

They're not just hiring us for the work. If they're hiring us as experts, they're hiring us to *make them feel safe enough* to confidently make decisions.

For example, in our Brandup, we only show one brand and a max of three logos. We also only show logos we think are perfect for their brand. Sometimes it actually kills us *not* to show certain logos that Steve made that we love, because they're just not *right*—even though they're really cool, and even if we know the client would love them.

We also don't show wildly *varied* logos. We do this to keep the decision-making to a minimum, and then we provide even more guardrails by giving them direction on *how to make the decisions.*

We tell them, for example, that *the goal is not for the client to like the logo.* The goal is for the logo to align with the brand's goals and, by extension, the business' goals.

Here's the psychology: humans hate uncertainty. It's wired in our brains from survival days, where wrong choices meant big risks. We fear losses, like bad decisions that could ruin a business, way more than we chase gains. Guardrails cut through that fear by creating a psychological safety net, a space where clients feel secure enough to make confident decisions quickly, without freezing. This also makes the process feel easier, as too many options can overwhelm the brain and lead to indecision paralysis. But presenting a clear path—for example, one brand, limited logos—simplifies the process, and makes clients feel seen and guided. This continues to build rapport and trust quickly, so that they continue to see you as a partner and leader, not a vendor. And then, when they follow your lead, they get better results *because* they're not second-guessing everything.

When developing an Intensive, always ask: *what guardrails can I put in place to ensure that clients can't accidentally undermine or derail the project that they are paying me to execute?*

The Three Pillars of a Successful Intensive

Running Intensives successfully comes down to **radical responsibility** for three things:

1. **Trust:** Most people treat trust as something passive; you earn it by doing a good job. But we build it deliberately. We take intentional steps to create trust at every stage because a client's trust directly affects effectiveness and profitability.

2. **Leadership:** If your clients are unpredictable, your timelines slip, or your projects drag on, it's because the client is leading, not you. The old saying "the client is always right" has trained us to hand over control. But clients come to us precisely *because* they're not sure what's right. True leadership means confidently guiding them through a process so seamless that following your lead feels effortless.
3. **Process:** Your process determines your profitability. If you're unprofitable, it's because your process is built on the false belief that time equals value. You quote based on how long you think something will take, then feel obligated to "do more" if you're paid more. That's a trap that hurts profitability, outcomes, and morale.

When you stop equating time with value, you can finally build a process based on outcomes, not hours. And when you do, your clients get better results—and you make more money in less time.

The Core Shift

At the heart of the Intensives Model is this message:

You hired us because you want us to show you the way—not to execute what's in your head.

Intensives are designed so that clients can relax into the process, feel engaged, and ultimately let go.

Design your Intensive

Disney It

For this, you'll want to use a process we call "Disney Mode." In the early days, Walt Disney famously separated imagination from execution. He hosted brainstorming meetings in a dedicated room where the sole purpose was to think big, without constraints or practicality, and where questioning or dismissing ideas was strictly forbidden.

Only afterward, in a different room and at a different time, would the team shift into analysis mode to assess feasibility and bring those ideas into reality.

Similarly, we love using Disney mode to free ourselves from the constraints of what's practical and what's possible.

To design your Intensive, start in Disney mode.

We are constrained by a lot of false assumptions about how things "usually" work, how we imagine people will act, and what we think things are supposed to look like. Intensives must start with a clean slate and use our imagination to build from scratch.

First, imagine your project without any constraints at all. It begins at 9 a.m. on a Monday morning. You have no other responsibilities, and neither does the client. Your full attention is on this one project all day today and tomorrow, and for however long it takes to complete. Map out the project exactly as it would happen if the client were fully available and able to provide anything you need, immediately and without interruption.

This exercise can feel challenging because many of the frustrations we've normalized are now invisible to us. When you're used to clients being slow to respond or unable to provide you with what's needed, it's difficult to even imagine a scenario where they show up prepared and deliver everything on time.

So, since you're reading this book and I'm not there to challenge you, you're going to need to notice and challenge yourself. While in Disney Mode, where are you *still* anticipating problems and creating a process for them? Stop. We are looking for magical, ideal processes, free of all obstacles, and we assume clients will have zero feedback, requests, or needs.

When we did this exercise, we identified that our ideal process was to gather all client information and collateral upfront, then move straight through the project to completion without interruption. Steve and I would design and build the brand, website, copy, and all related materials in one focused stretch, then hand them over to the client, fully finished, live, and ready to launch.

After you've mapped out the flawless, ideal version of your project, you can use it as the blueprint for your Intensive. Identify the points where that "Disney version" could break down in real life, and put processes in place to preempt those challenges before they arise.

With that foundation in place, let's walk through the key principles and assumptions that will help you design these systems effectively.

Assume The Client Won't Do Their HW
The first approach is to assume that when you give clients a task or homework, they won't reliably do it. Few people in this world, myself included, get every task on their plate done on

time. Most of us are constantly rearranging our priority lists. And if your request is not a top priority, then it will usually get moved down the list.

So let's build that assumption directly into the process. If your work depends on clients—or multiple stakeholders—gathering information or completing a detailed intake, you need systems that remove uncertainty. The first strategy comes straight from the Lead Product Method: make the intake requirements explicit before the contract is signed. Set a firm due date and clearly state that the project will not proceed as scheduled if the intake isn't received. Say it on the call, reinforce it in writing, and confirm it again once the contract and deposit are submitted. For most clients, that clarity alone is enough.

When I ask for the intake by Monday, I send a reminder a few days before—usually Thursday or Friday—to check whether they're stuck on anything. If I sense a pattern of lateness, I don't rely solely on reminders. I scheduled a meeting on the due date itself, with the understanding that if the intake isn't submitted beforehand, we'll use that time to complete it live. We can sit quietly on Zoom while they work, but the time is protected. If a client struggles with structure, I simply provide it.

This becomes even more valuable with larger organizations, where information often needs to come from people you don't directly manage. Those stakeholders may not fully grasp the project's scope or consider your intake urgent. But when your process requires them to attend a kickoff call that exists specifically to carve out time for intake, you remove the ambiguity. One intentional hour upfront can save you weeks of follow-ups, delays, and frustration later.

Take Everything Off Their Plate

Another principle of Intensives that has helped me tremendously is the idea that we really don't want our clients to have to do much at all. Wherever I can, I have taken things off their plate. Sometimes that means developing a new skill—and it's very likely one that will serve you well in the long term.

Early on in our branding process, I didn't write the copy because I wasn't a copywriter. Clients either had to hire a copywriter or write it themselves. I learned quickly that they struggled to make this happen. They either had trouble finding someone or, if they didn't want to pay for it, struggled even more to write the copy themselves because this was obviously not their area of expertise.

The time I spent chasing clients for copy was holding up our projects. So out of frustration more than anything, I finally just started doing this myself.

You might be starting to imagine the things that you could theoretically take off your client's plate, but are questioning whether you *should* because it's not your zone of genius. Here are my thoughts on that.

When I started writing copy for clients, I was just okay at it, and I also wasn't charging professional copywriting prices. In fact, I was including it in the project's price. So my clients were getting a huge value without having to pay for it. The value wasn't just the copy; it was the act of taking it off their plate. And because I was doing this for so many clients, I developed the skills and became a copywriter, which greatly increased the value of what I could offer my clients and became a huge asset in my own business.

I quickly saw how much more effective and efficient our projects were when I owned this step instead of waiting for, or pestering, clients to complete it. And because copywriting wasn't listed as a separate line item with its own price tag, clients almost always accepted it without hesitation.

That distinction is critical. When packages are priced around deliverables and hours, clients tend to view copywriting as optional—something they think they can do themselves to save money. But when it's simply included because you know it improves the outcome and streamlines the process, it rarely gets questioned. It doesn't feel like an "add-on" because you haven't positioned it as one. Over time, this kind of repetition—working with similar clients and seeing the same patterns—builds real expertise. You begin to anticipate what will and won't work before problems arise, and that foresight significantly strengthens your authority in the client's eyes.

So ask yourself: where can I take something off my client's plate? How can I require the absolute minimum from them?

Control the Intake Process
When you're thinking about everything you must get from the client, the question now becomes: how can I create a schedule and clear communication from the very beginning, including consequences if they don't meet deadlines, to ensure that whatever they have to do will be as easy as possible and done on time?

Sometimes it's as simple as collecting more information, logins, or photos, but for larger clients, you may need feedback from multiple people, such as *their* clients or key stakeholders. These are the processes that usually slow projects down and make them drag out over months, simply because people's schedules are so hard to wrangle.

Here's how you avoid that. You again set the expectation before they even sign off on the project by saying something like, "I am going to dedicate three days to these interviews—and only these three days. I'll need you to communicate that to the people I'm interviewing, so that they can pick their slots up front and commit to that day and time."

Setting that expectation changes how people show up. Once you've set a clear boundary around those three days, it becomes the project leader's job to ensure everyone involved schedules accordingly.

It's not always perfect, but even if one or two of those stakeholders are completely unavailable during those three days, just getting *most* of them on a schedule makes a huge difference. And the two people who can't will be more amenable to making it happen because you will make it clear they are asking for an exception.

By having this kind of clear-cut communication and process from the beginning, you are setting up a dynamic where the client *wants* to follow your process.

Complete the Project Upfront

It can feel daunting to fully step into the role of project leader. This is often where imposter syndrome kicks in. I have had to learn how to hold that weight, knowing that what I present is what the client will ultimately get. Because of the process I use and the way I lead from the very beginning, the outcome rests largely on my judgment.

That is a hell of a lot of responsibility!

But when you *trust yourself* to deliver the best outcome, you don't need constant input from the client. I see many providers ask for feedback at every step before they move forward, not because they truly need it, but because they are afraid of committing too fully to a direction without the client's approval.

I get it. No one wants to spend weeks building something only to find out it is completely wrong.

Here is the mindset shift this requires. If you do thorough discovery up front, ask the right questions, and you are *genuinely more qualified to solve the problem than the client*, then your leadership will produce a better result than if the client leads the project.

In that case, the most valuable thing you can do is take the work off their plate and move forward without asking for approval at every step.

That level of confidence takes practice. It is a muscle that gets stronger with more reps. But when you build it, you deliver higher value work more efficiently.

Steve and I design brands and websites using Gestalt thinking. Each piece matters, but no single piece matters more than the whole.

The effectiveness of the work comes from how everything fits together, not from (in our line of work) whether a specific pixel or font size is perfect in isolation.

When we used to spread projects out over multiple weeks and presentations—asking for feedback and reassurance at every step—we often ended up with clients choosing a final logo before the brand itself was even designed. That changed completely once we started delivering the entire project at once. We realized the logo belongs later in the process, as one expression of the brand, not the thing that defines it. Looking back, that earlier approach feels disjointed. If a brand is meant to work together to convey a cohesive personality and presence, shouldn't it be developed and evaluated as a whole?

That belief was reinforced during a project in which we presented three logos alongside the full brand design. The client loved one of the logos personally, but ultimately chose another because it best aligned with the brand's overall vibe. Seeing everything together allowed him to make a business decision instead of defaulting to personal taste—something he likely wouldn't have done without that context. The power of showing the full vision at once shows up everywhere. Even when Steve shows me unfinished work and asks for feedback, it's hard to respond meaningfully when I can't see where he's headed. I can't see what he is imagining, and that gap creates confusion.

Yet we do this to clients all the time, asking them to approve work before they can see the full picture. It's an unfair request!

This approach might not seem directly applicable to every industry on its face, yet there are almost always opportunities to go further upfront, show more at a time, and get approval faster. Students who have implemented this—whether they're designers, copywriters, marketers, coaches, or consultants—has been amazed when they try it and have the same experience. When clients see the full end result, and it's *better* than what they hoped for or imagined, you can get an excited "yes" and approval on what is usually a multi-part project in one meeting. It often just takes the guts to try it and the confidence to go further based on your expertise, rather than requiring approval along the way.

So ask yourself: Where are you asking for feedback or approval before you truly need it? If you trusted yourself more and led more confidently, could you move forward without stopping? And if you knew the client would ultimately approve it, why not continue?

Do It Live

Another key to really effective Intensives is the live component. One thing that changed the game for us when it came to revisions was presenting all of our work live. Design, website, copy—never again would I email work out to a client for them to view on their own time.

Because presenting live is not just about giving them the actual work. It's about creating buy-in, inciting enthusiasm, and continuing to build that trust.

A process I developed for presenting work that gets buy-in on a whole bunch of decisions at once is something I call **Magic Hour**. This is what I do for the first presentation of the work for our clients. At this point, they have already paid in full and have seen *nothing*, so this is a big reveal showing them the full brand, pitching the logo, and sharing the main messaging and copy. It's giving a full picture of what the outcome is going to look like. This is a key moment because it solidifies their trust in us and gets them excited for the rest. It's also where we get approval on most of the big decisions, and once this is done, the rest of the project is usually a breeze.

Magic Hour is one of the most important ingredients in a successful Intensive. So let's break down what it is and why it's so effective.

The Five Principles of Magic Hour

The Magic Hour is the first big reveal of your work. It's when all your strategy, creativity, and brilliance meet the client's eyes for the first time.

It's also the moment that solidifies their buy-in and solidifies *your* role as the captain.

When you lead it well, it becomes one of the most satisfying, empowering moments of your entire process.

There are five key principles to make that happen.

1. Start with WHY

We all know Simon Sinek's famous book and TED Talk—S*tart with Why.*

He talks about how people connect with a brand, not based on what it delivers but why it matters. But this principle applies just as much to how clients connect with *your* ideas.

Too often, creative professionals start their presentations with *what* they did—"Here's the logo," "Here's the layout," "Here's the campaign." They expect the work to speak for itself, that the client will see its brilliance on their own. But just because a client has already hired you doesn't mean they're sold on everything you're about to show them.

In fact, it's the opposite. The selling doesn't stop—it simply shifts. Instead of selling the work itself, you're continually selling confidence: in you, in your thinking, and in the decision they already made to work with you. Every presentation either strengthens or weakens that belief.

So before you show a single deliverable, reconnect them to the reason they started this journey in the first place. Remind them *why* they came to you, and *why* this matters to them and their dreams. This way, when you present the work directly after, you can tie it back to the outcome they *really* want. Sharing the why up front ensures it's top of mind and frames the decision-making process. In the same way we used "so that" statements to connect the strategy we're presenting to the results clients want in the LP, we're doing it live here as we present the work.

That primes their brain to receive your ideas with the right context.

2. Breadcrumb the ideas

If you've ever watched the Olympics, you know they don't just show athletes competing. They show you the backstory—the childhood training, the early mornings, the heartbreaks and comebacks. Because once you understand where someone came from, you start rooting for them. You're invested in their story and their success.

That's the experience we also want to create in Magic Hour.

Never drop finished work and assume it will speak for itself. Even when the work is exceptional, clients won't experience it with the same clarity you do without guidance. Your job is to help them see what you see.

Instead, take them on the journey of your process: how you got there, and why you made the decisions you made. Share your thinking, and even the challenges you had, the choices you had to make, and why you made them.

When clients understand the evolution of the work, they come to see why the solution you provided *is* the right solution for them.

And they will actually root for your solution! Because they've become invested in the story of it.

When the story of the thinking is breadcrumbed throughout the presentation, and they agree with your thinking, it eliminates all of the noise that often fills clients' heads, where they start wondering: wait, did you think about this? Or that? Did you consider this idea over here?

Those are the questions that tend to live in a client's mind when you don't explain your thinking. Most of the time, it comes back to that fear of making a mistake. Clients often feel it is their responsibility to ask whether you have thought through certain details because they believe they're being diligent. If you don't show them how much thought went into your work, and how each decision connects back to their goals, they will fill in the gaps themselves. At best, those assumptions are unhelpful.

3. Sell the Dream
Most people present work in phases. In branding, that usually means moodboards, logos, wireframes, homepages, and so

on—seeking approval at each step.

But that's like trying to sell a house by showing the buyer the upstairs bathroom, then the kitchen cabinets, then the dining room molding.

When we buy a house, we don't buy the parts—*we buy the dream*. We imagine our life inside the whole house, how it will feel, and who we will be.

It's the same with your client's brand or business.

Don't show them fragments and make them piece the vision together. Paint the whole picture and let them see the full transformation. Let them *feel* what it will be like to live inside this new identity, this new business, this new possibility.

That's what moves people from "I like it" to "I need this."

4. Feed Them Spinach

Remember Popeye? He'd pop open a can of spinach, down it in one gulp, and suddenly become ten times stronger.

Before you ask your clients to make a decision, you need to give them that spinach—the "power" and confidence to do it.

Whenever you ask someone to make a big decision, their fear of making the *wrong* one kicks in. This is usually what prompts them to ask for more time to think about it or to show it to others for their opinion.

If you can give them that boost in that very moment, and assure them that *they have everything they need* to make a confident decision, their wavering and worrying will disappear.

This means giving them advice on *how* to think about the decision and permission to make it. Giving them safety by showing them that you already did the due diligence of considering everything, and that there is no wrong answer here.

I will literally say to clients, "We did all of the work and exploration, so you don't have to. We created and explored dozens of logos, and we are only showing you the three that we think hit the mark and fulfill the goals of this project. These are all approved by Steve and me, and we are only showing you work that fulfills the project goals, **so you cannot make a wrong decision here.**"

And when you say this, say it all with absolute confidence, because you know what you are presenting is right for them.

5. Expect "David's Nose."

There's a famous story about Michelangelo sculpting *David*.

When the commissioner came to see the nearly finished statue, he was thrilled—except that he suggested the nose could be a little smaller.

So Michelangelo climbed up the scaffolding and dramatically chipped away a bit of dust with his chisel.

"Better now?" he asked.

"Perfect," the man said.

We call that *David's Nose Syndrome.*

Most clients need to leave their mark on the work in some way. It's how they feel ownership.

So we can actually expect it, even look for it, and invite it.

We expect them to ask to see the logo with one tiny tweak, like bumping up the font a couple of sizes. Half the time, once they see it, they still go back to the original.

That small moment of collaboration allows them to walk away proud, satisfied, and taking full ownership of the work.

Sometimes it helps them *believe* in it even more. And their belief and conviction will make the outcome *more valuable to them.*

We use Magic Hour to present our creative work, yet the principles can be applied to presenting everything from financial advice to a coaching plan to a consulting strategy.

Our Magic Hour presentation usually runs between forty-five minutes to an hour and a half, but the framework works just as well for a five or ten-minute presentation. You can move people through this process very quickly. In fact, I use these principles to run most meetings because they set expectations, align everyone on why we are there, and put us on the same path from the start.

Even if the work you're presenting is small, you can still use the framing. Explain why the work exists, how it connects to the goals, what decisions you made, and what you chose not to do. If decisions are required, you can also explain how a decision should be made.

One of my favorite strategies for helping clients feel confident saying yes is not asking for feedback or opinions at all, but simply asking, "Are you good with this?" When we truly nail it, most clients say yes with no revisions.

When we ask for opinions, on the other hand, we often invite people to provide feedback that may not be necessary. Asking "Are you good with this?" gives clients permission to simply agree.

Of course, expect that they may want to tweak a word or sentence—just a bit of *David's Nose* to the work. This process applies to whatever you are presenting. The only thing that changes is the amount of detail you include.

Beliefs That Will Stop You

Now that you've seen how to design an Intensive and dramatically reduce delivery time, let's talk about the resistance that usually shows up next: charging a high price for a shorter project.

This is the most common pushback I hear when I talk about intensifying a process. Many people instinctively lengthen projects to justify higher prices because so many of us were taught that *value and price* are tied to *time and effort*. I did this myself in the early days. When we raised our prices, we also stretched our timelines to justify the increase.

The logic went something like this: Steve, our two employees, and I were going to work on this project for five months. There would be multiple meetings, phases, and deliverables. *That's* why it costs $30,000.

At the time, the idea of delivering the same outcome in two days would have felt impossible. Why would anyone pay that much for something done so quickly?

Here's why:

There's a famous story about Picasso sitting in a café in Paris when a woman recognized him.

Thrilled, she rushed over, gushing about how much she admired his work, and asked if he'd sign her napkin.

Picasso smiled, picked up the napkin, and instead of just signing it, he drew a quick little sketch. Then he handed it back and said, "That'll be ten thousand francs."

The woman was shocked. "Ten thousand francs?! But it only took you five minutes!"

Picasso smiled again, took the napkin back, and said, "No, madame—it took me a lifetime."

That story is the perfect reminder that the value of what we create isn't in the minutes it takes to make—it's in the lifetime it took to *acquire the skills to do it*.

Most of us have been trained to believe that when a client pays us a lot of money, they're paying for our *time*. That's why we price by the hour, or the week, or the number of deliverables. We think time equals effort and effort equals worth.

But the truth is, the value in creative work isn't in how long it takes you to do it. The value is in the experience, the discernment, and the *eye* that makes it possible for you to do it well.

Whether it takes you three hours to find the perfect color or thirty seconds to spot it instantly, the value to the client is the same. Whether you think about their problem and mull it over for days, or you immediately see what can change to solve it, shouldn't matter to the client at all. The value is that you can solve it.

What they're paying for is not how long you spend—it's how *right* you get it.

And I get it. That's easy to understand in theory and hard to believe in your body.

Because so many of us were raised to equate effort with integrity.

But that belief keeps you stuck working longer than necessary to prove your worth.

Let me put it another way: If a corporate consultant hired us to design their logo, and Steve spent weeks hand-painting an original piece of art for it, would that make it more valuable than a clean, modern wordmark he could design in an hour?

Of course not. It would actually be *less* valuable because it would be *wrong*.

That consultant doesn't want an art piece. They want a brand that positions them as a credible expert. A hand-painted logo might be beautiful, but it would miss the mark completely.

Time does not equal value. Value comes from knowing what's right and having the confidence to deliver it simply, clearly, and quickly.

Think about how long it took you to deliver great results earlier in your career. You were still building the skills, experience, and confidence you needed. As you gained expertise, it took you *less* time to deliver the same results, or even better ones.

So why do we accept the idea that, for a project to be worth more money, it should take more time?

If I want the best outcome, I want the person who can get me there most effectively. That person usually has enough experience to move faster than someone who is still figuring it out.

This is why experts often raise their hourly rates over time. But there is always a ceiling to that model. And personally, I refuse to pay anyone by the hour. I don't want to reward someone for taking *longer*. The only thing that should truly matter to your clients is the end result. That's what they're hiring you for! If it takes longer than expected, I wouldn't want to pay *more* for that inefficiency.

The kind of clients you want feel the same way. Any client

who is focused on your time is focused on the wrong thing. That might sound like a client problem, but most of the time it is a communication problem. If you focus on time, you teach *them* to focus on time, too.

I have coached people who are afraid to package their services because they do not trust themselves to stay within a set timeframe. So they charge by the hour instead, which means the client ends up paying more simply because the provider cannot manage their own time.

And here's where hourly rates can go the other way. A friend of mine launched a podcast and was looking to hire an editor. The editor said she charged $100 an hour. My friend had a limited budget, and she was worried the hours would add up, and asked the editor to agree to $100 dollars per episode if they didn't need any content editing.

At first, that felt like a win. But over time, my friend started to feel resentful, even ripped off, because she realized each episode was now only taking about fifteen minutes to edit. She only felt that way because the editor framed her work as hourly. If the editor had simply said, "I edit podcasts for $100 per episode," my friend would never have questioned the value.

This is the problem with tying time to money.

Because people *do* naturally think in hourly terms, it's your job as the expert to help them focus on the thing that matters: the outcomes.

This is why Intensives work so well. They are outcome-focused, and they deliver another layer of value people deeply care about: speed. We live in a world that values fast solutions. As long as speed does not compromise results, people will pay *more* for it, not less.

If a client came to you and said, "I know this usually takes three months, but I need it done in two weeks," you would feel entitled to a rush fee, wouldn't you? So what is the difference between that and building a process that delivers the same result faster by design?

The resistance to this model comes from an internal belief that excellence requires time, effort, and even exhaustion. Many of us equate *hard work* with *value*. Working faster can feel like cutting corners. You may even feel guilty charging more for something that takes you *less* time.

I once had a student who instantly knew how to fix a potential client's e-commerce issue. She told them exactly what plugin to install and solved the problem on the spot. The client was thrilled. But the student felt awkward charging for it because it was so obvious to her.

It was only obvious because she had spent *years* building that knowledge. The value was not the time it took to say it; it was knowing what to say.

It's like calling a plumber who immediately knows which valve to turn off to stop a leak. The value is not the minutes it takes. It is the knowledge of which knob to twist.

Many people discount their value when it feels easy to them. But a skill never starts out as easy. You earned that ease through learning, failures, repetition, and persistence.

You may worry that clients will not accept this. That they *want* projects stretched out. Often, that belief comes from *years* of managing work defensively, waiting on approvals, feedback, and validation.

But the root of this is usually fear. Fear of asserting authority and your opinions, and then being wrong or being disliked.

Many wanna-be experts are more invested in being *liked* than being *trusted*. But true experts are guided by the project's goals and feel more beholden to the outcome than to being liked by the client, because they were hired for the result, not a friend, and they take pride in that mission. Clients who also care about the outcome want to be led, and they will thank you for taking control.

Ultimately, I think the real fear is rejection. What if you tighten boundaries, lead the process, and they say no?

One of two things usually happens: either you celebrate that you just dodged a bullet, because a client who can't respect your boundaries is going to be a nightmare client. Or you turn them into an amazing client.

Here's what happened when one of our students held firm with a difficult client, in her own words:

"Two weeks ago, I had a Fit Call with one of 'those' potential clients, the kind who says they're "all in" but then starts emailing you about how they'd like to tweak the way you work. He was totally on board with The LP, loved it, wanted it, but before he'd even booked, he was trying to schedule it at night, on a Sunday, while rearranging what would come after it and what we'd deliver, when, and how, before we'd even gotten into anything.

I could feel him pulling at the edges of my boundaries, and the old me might have bent (definitely would've bent!). Old me would've thought, "Oh, he's had a hard time. Maybe if I'm flex-

ible, he'll like me more." Old me would've worked later, shifted things around, justified it to myself as "good customer service," and quietly seethed.

But I don't do that anymore.

I stayed calm, polite, and *firm*. Explained that this is how we work, and if it doesn't fit, that's totally fine, no hard feelings.

He didn't like that much, sent a slightly passive-aggressive "never mind, we'll take our business elsewhere" email.

And tbh, I was *furious*, I'd done nothing wrong, offered plenty of flexibility, and still somehow ended up being painted as the unhelpful one!!

But I let it go, walked the dog, and moved on.

A couple of days ago, he emailed again.

His circumstances have changed; he's also spoken to other agencies, liked them, but none of them had the *level* of big-picture thinking or perspective we had. And he's ready to do it *properly*, **on my terms.**

It was such a satisfying reminder that holding your boundaries isn't rude, it's *everything*, and when you stand firm, the right ones don't run; they regroup, respect you, and come back ready.

So if you're in that stage where a client's asking for "just a little tweak" to how you work, **hold your ground**, you're not being awkward, you're being professional, and somewhere down the line, you'll get the same email I did that starts, *"I've had a think..."*

If you struggle with having clear boundaries, this might be hard at first. This student is a (self-identified) recovering people-pleaser, which makes this story so powerful. If she can do it, you can do it. It's just a matter of practice and developing the muscles and the stomach.

Once you start holding firm boundaries and realize they actually provide more value to your clients, they'll appreciate it, you'll get better results, and you'll want to lean into it.

But you have to cross the chasm of even wanting to try in the first place.

Maybe you'd like to try, but you're convinced this won't work for you because of your industry or clients. Your business is special. Your clients are different.

I'm not saying that certain industries and certain kinds of clients are not more difficult than others. But what I really hear is that there's comfort in thinking that you are the exception.

What do you get out of believing that this doesn't work for you and your specific situation? Well, you get to keep feeling justified when your projects take longer than they should.

And you don't have to take responsibility for the fact that you're working more than you'd like and not making as much money. Yeah, I said it. Just because you can't tighten your process into two Intensive days as I do doesn't mean you can't greatly reduce the time and BS in your current process.

For the first couple of years we were doing this process, every agency owner I told about it said, *"That's not possible."* It wasn't possible *until* we started doing it. And now, hundreds of people do it this way.

This is your opportunity to be a pioneer in your industry. The one who thought, "It won't work here," and then made it happen.

Shift in Thinking: Clients Crave Direction

Clients don't actually want weeks to mull over your work. They want you to lead them to decisions they feel confident in.

Our copywriter for interior designers Deb Mitchell learned this the hard way—and it transformed her business. She used to struggle with *so much BS* around feedback and revisions—clients would take weeks, months, or even longer to get their revisions back to her so she could make their final changes and wrap their project (and often collect their final payment).

Deb wasn't sure her clients—who were used to treating copy like a life-or-death choice—would buy into the Intensives process and Magic Hour. She wasn't sure how she could get her clients to stop treating their copy like it was a major life decision that they needed to sit on for ages, and give real-time feedback instead.

She developed an Intensives process that worked for her, shrinking the projects down from months to three weeks. Using Magic Hour's trust-building language and posture, she now runs live feedback sessions, and clients *love it*. Not only do they *not* ask for the document so they can mull over the changes they want; they ask for very few edits and many have *zero* changes.

Deb got rid of the endless waiting, extensive emails back and forth, and stalled payments. Now, projects wrap fast, clients feel led, and her mental health thanks her.

That's the shift: lead with guardrails, and clients follow. They don't need time to second-guess. They need you to make decisions that feel safe.

Take Action:

1. **What's one piece of BS in your current process that exists only because you're afraid of what the client might think?** Be brutally honest. Are you offering endless revisions because you think they want them—or because you're scared they won't be happy? Are you stretching timelines to justify your price? That fear is costing you profit and peace.
2. **When was the last time a project took longer than you planned—and what could you have done differently upfront to prevent it?** Look back at your most recent stalled project. Were you asking the client to do a bunch of work upfront that you could have either done for them or walked them through live to make sure you received it on time? Were you asking for opinions instead of decisions? Showing fragments instead of the full vision? Leading like a vendor instead of a captain? Each of these is an opportunity to tighten up.
3. **What would your "Disney Mode" version of your ideal project look like?** Forget all constraints. The client shows up ready, you have everything you need, and there are no obstacles, there's no waiting, and no scope creep. Map it out. Then ask: what's actually stopping me from getting closer to this? (Hint: it's probably not the client—it's *how you're leading them.*)

If You Only Take One Thing From This Chapter:

Stop pricing like your time is the product. You're not selling hours—you're selling the outcome only you can deliver because of the lifetime it took to know how. And the more skilled you become, the more valuable and shorter the projects will be.

PART FIVE

No BS Money Mindset

Have you ever chased something you were sure would change how you felt—only to get it and realize nothing really changed at all?

When we first started our business, we just wanted to pay for our lifestyle. $10,000/month was our stretch goal, and it felt far out of reach. But after officially launching our business in March 2011, we hit our first $10,000 month that August.

I couldn't believe it! I felt so giddy and successful.

That lasted for about a minute. As exciting as it was, I immediately also felt unsteady. Sure, we did $10,000 this month, but could we do it *again*? And even when I did—month after month—I never really felt secure about it. I was always stressed about what would come next.

A monthly goal meant I was starting from zero again on the first of every month, like a nightmare Groundhog Day situation.

And while I was thrilled to reach that first goal in just six months, you have to remember—it was me and Steve, working *more* than full-time, hustling our butts off just to make $10,000 a month, which, in New York City, is middle-class *if* you don't need vacations, savings, or space.

We generated more revenue each year as we got savvier, but by March 2014, we were still $40,000 in debt with nothing in the bank. No matter how much we made those first three years, it never felt like *enough*. Even when I exceeded my goal, there was always the fear that next month, I wouldn't.

Of course, I was even *more* stressed when we went into debt. I'd jolt awake at 2:30am, mind racing through everything I *should* be doing to find just one more project to generate some cash and create a little bit of breathing room. I believed that if only we could make more money, *that* would alleviate this knot in my stomach and solve all my problems.

I soon found out how wrong I was.

Less than nine months later, we were on that three-week vacation in Hawaii in a completely different financial situation. We had been incredibly busy with work since the summer. We had been taking every client that came to us, doing multiple Brandups a week, and stacking cash. We had more *money in the bank than I had ever seen before*, and clients were booking months in advance to work with us.

And... *my stress hadn't gone away!*

Here I was, having made significant financial gains. I had paid off all our debt. I had saved a pile of money. I had even saved money for taxes! I was able to pay for and take three weeks off for a vacation, disconnected from any work. We even had clients booked for when we returned.

How could I still be worried? This was the *exact* situation that I thought would finally relieve my stress!

It took me a few more years to really understand why.

Fast forward to 2019. We had just moved into a much bigger, two-bedroom apartment due to our growing family. Our rent had *quadrupled* overnight from $1,500/month to $6,000/month.

Despite the higher overhead (or perhaps because of it), we decided to pull back from client work and invest full-time in a program that promised to teach us how to scale our thousand-dollar online course into a million-dollar-a-year income stream.

We had tried selling our online course in different ways for a few years, and we had already generated a few hundred thousand dollars from it, so it seemed like a bet worth taking. We spent the first three months of 2019 working around the clock, learning the course material and doing everything the coach taught us.

But by April of 2019, we had accumulated $100,000 in debt on a bunch of credit cards. That was the most money I'd ever owed (by 2.5x), and it was definitely scary.

Yet here's what's really interesting: I wasn't *nearly* as stressed out as I'd been back in 2014 when we owed less than half that. I was actually less stressed than I'd been while vacationing in Hawaii with a bunch of money in the bank!

How could that be? The stakes were much higher now with a young child and higher overhead, plus we owed a significant amount of money.

That's when I learned, in real time, that *feeling* financially free has less to do with how much cash you have in the bank or even how much money you have coming in at that exact moment...

...and much more to do with **your confidence in your ability to make money.**

Which tracked with the stories I heard growing up. My dad was an accountant for over 30 years; he often shared anecdotes about how some of his wealthiest clients were still so cheap and miserable. They seemed *terrified* about losing their money.

What I heard from him, and then experienced firsthand, was that having money not only does *not* relieve us of financial stress, but it can often trigger people to worry *more* about losing it.

A friend of mine has a very good friend worth almost a billion dollars. She once told me that, despite all his money, he doesn't feel financially secure either. Does that sound crazy to you? You're probably thinking: "I'd feel financially secure with a *fraction* of that."

When you don't have enough to cover your basic lifestyle, it can be hard to understand, and you might have to go through the same experience I did to finally see for yourself. But if you'd like me to save you the trouble, here's what I think will benefit you: if you don't feel financially secure now, you won't feel financially secure with $X dollars in the bank, either.

Whatever that number is for you, your brain will naturally start to fixate on potential *loss*, rather than *abundance*.

This reminds me of a game I played in a behavioral economics class I took back in college. Each of us sat at a separate computer as an anonymous player and started with $10 in our account. We were paired up, anonymously, and given the option to keep our $10, or send our money to the other player. If we sent it, the system would triple the amount before giving it to the other person—so if I sent $10, they'd get $30.

Here's the catch: if both players sent their $10, we'd each end up with $30. But if I sent it and they didn't, I'd lose my $10 while they'd keep theirs *and* get my $30. On paper, the best outcome for both of us was obvious: send the money, cooperate, and everyone wins.

But as we continued to play the game, it became clear that, more often than not, people chose to keep their $10. Losing $10 just felt worse than potentially gaining $20.

This is thanks to an evolutionary survival instinct that flags resources as temporary. When you hit a financial goal, the brain doesn't celebrate; it kicks into **loss aversion mode**, a cognitive bias identified by psychologists like Daniel Kahneman and Amos Tversky. The pain of *losing* $1 outweighs the joy of *gaining* $1 by nearly two-to-one. So, having cash can trigger heightened anxiety about protecting it, making you feel *less*, not more, secure.

This also connects to the **hedonic treadmill**—no matter how much cash you have in the bank, your baseline worry resets; "more" never feels enough. Studies, such as those in the Journal of Economic Psychology, show that financial security isn't achieved by acquiring a fixed amount of savings, but a psychological state based on perceived control and certainty about the future.

Chasing "more" keeps stress alive because the brain wants certainty, and an ever-moving goal post can never provide it. This stress is even worse for those of us who are self-employed without the perceived safety of a steady paycheck (which is not without its own risk, since no job is guaranteed forever.)

The Elusive Search for "Steady"

When I ask entrepreneurs how much they want to make, they almost always respond with a *monthly* number. I did too, for a long time—our world has taught us to think in months.

We pay our rent or mortgage monthly, our credit card bills are due monthly, our utilities and internet and insurance premiums are paid monthly. When we were salaried employees, we were paid every two weeks. So when we go out on our own, it's natural to bring that desire for "steady" with us.

This is why many small businesses covet the retainer model. The dream of having one or multiple clients guaranteed to pay a monthly fee feels like it alleviates some of that stress; you're no longer starting your month at zero, hustling to make your nut every 30 days. You've got at least some or all of your bills paid just from the retainer clients you have.

This fantasy, however, can be short-lived—and it's often a farce.

Let me tell you about Rhonda (name changed to protect her privacy) because her story is one I've heard *dozens* of times.

Rhonda left her corporate job to go out on her own, and her first client was her former boss. She went from employed to getting paid as a consultant at $10,000 a month. She quickly landed a second client at the same rate, and worked with those two clients for over a year, generating $240,000 annually.

"This owning a business thing is easy!" she said to herself. "What's everyone complaining about?"

Then one day, her old boss told her they'd be bringing her job in-house, and they gave her 30 days' notice. During that month, the second client also decided to end their engagement. Within 60 days, she went from collecting $20,000/month to having no clients and no income coming in.

This is when Rhonda started to panic, because you know what she was doing to build her business while working for those two clients for over a year?

Nothing.

Nothing to market herself, nothing to build her pipeline, nothing to position herself as an authority in the marketplace.

She mistook what she had—two part-time jobs—for owning a business.

When you have a job, part-time or full-time, someone else pays you to work for them. That's it.

When you have a *business* (one able to sustainably support you and generate a profit), delivering the goods for your clients is only *half* your job. The other half is servicing your most important client: *your business.* That means marketing, sales, and product development. It's the reason I developed and teach the 50/25/25 formula: to make sure that business owners plan for this, instead of leaving it as an afterthought.

Because a business without marketing and sales is just a job.

When your time is filled with one or multiple retainer clients, and you're not investing at least 25% to 50% of your time in marketing, sales, and product development (YOU and your process are the product here), you have a part- or full-time job. Except without any benefits. And with even less safety, since it's easier to be let go by a retainer client than by a boss—after all, if you're fired as an employee, you can generally collect severance and/or unemployment.

This is one reason I rail against retainers for expert-led businesses. While they seem to offer a steady income stream, all they truly do is give business owners a false sense of security. When your bills are covered by your retainer work, and your work hours are pretty much filled with fulfilling those contracts, how much effort are you *really* going to put into keeping your pipeline full, marketing your services, building your audience, and even improving on your process?

Most people become complacent and leave those efforts on the "nice to do when I have time" list. Except they only finally get around to it when they're in panic mode, following the sudden departure of their retainer clients. That's when they realize they have no real business to speak of.

Here's another catch: most retainer projects are inherently unprofitable. When negotiating, most businesses aren't charging a premium for their time, and most clients are looking for a deal as the trade-off for paying on an ongoing basis. I've seen hundreds of students join our program with at least a few retainer contracts. When they pop those numbers into our Freedom Calculator, the retainer clients are never profitable enough to support their financial goals.

This unprofitable relationship is made even worse by the fact that scope creep is hard to avoid in retainers. You depend on your retainer clients, so you don't want to lose them. And when they inevitably ask for extra stuff here and there, or just reach out regularly, you naturally act quickly to help. The threat of disappointing them in any way—and possibly losing this income stream—makes it hard to maintain boundaries.

Naturally, this kind of ongoing relationship is also antithetical to the efficiency we talked about in the last chapter. With multiple retainers, most people are usually jumping from client to client all day, losing a lot of efficiency with context switching.

Now, I'm in full support of any retainer client that isn't guilty of the above sins. If you have a retainer relationship (1) that's profitable enough to support your financial and freedom goals, (2) whose scope is managed and boundaries are clear, and (3) where you're dedicated to minding your business as your most important client, go for it. (One way to do that is the Intensive retainer model that I shared in the last chapter.)

But do not fall prey to chasing the false security of retainer clients and then confusing full-time work for them with owning a business.

You might be wondering: "How do I know the difference, especially when I'm just starting out?"

First, we need to talk about what it means to be a business owner.

Real talk: There's no small business that will allow you to *completely* check out and just sustain or keep growing without you. Certainly not in the world of selling expertise.

And second, as Peter Drucker said: *[in business] if you're not growing, you're dying.* Even thriving businesses are like plants; stop watering them and they'll eventually wither away.

No matter how solid your business is, it's still at the whim of market forces, changes in your life, changes in tastes, changes in marketing, and changes in your industry. There is no true *set-it-and-forget-it* service-based business.

Nothing is guaranteed; there will always be a need to stay current and competitive, and small businesses will always be subject to some kind of rollercoaster, even when you're incredibly successful and/or have a team that's doing all the work for you.

Once we accept this assumption, we can work with it.

It's important to shift your perspective on what retainers truly are: they're clients who say they *intend* to keep paying you. That doesn't mean they will, even with a contract. So if you want actual security, you must *operate* as if they can leave at any time, *even if* they've agreed to pay you for a longer timeframe.

It doesn't mean being stressed; it means being prepared and ready for when (not if!) it happens.

I remember hearing Alex Hormozi, a well-known entrepreneur, marketer, and investor, describe an observation he made while hanging out with some of the world's biggest business titans, like Richard Branson. He said that, given the scale of their operations, these guys were being sued by a dozen people and had tons of fires blazing around them at any moment.

Yet they stay steady and unfazed.

And of course they do; they wouldn't have their empires if every challenge knocked them off their feet, rattled them, and took them out of the game for even a short period of time.

In contrast, so many of us are like a reed blowing in the

wind, with feelings largely determined by what's been going on recently, or even that day. Someone you thought was going to hire you said they decided to go another way? We feel bad. Just made an unexpected sale? We feel great! When I used to take sales calls for my company, my mood was largely determined by how my calls went on any given day.

But that's no way to live—and it's not doing your business any favors, either.

Because when we feel lousy, it affects everything we do. It affects how we show up when we're talking to potential clients and referral partners about our business. We think we're good at hiding it, and maybe we are, but people can tell when someone is authentically confident in what they do and what they offer, and it matters.

This is not a binary shift, by the way. Have a crappy day, and feel your feelings, by all means! But if you want more of the things you want in your business, you've got to get rid of this unnecessary "head trash" weighing you down and preventing you from giving your business the best version of yourself.

How to Think Annually

A huge adjustment that made a big difference in how I felt about money and financial security was my shift to what I call *Annual Thinking.*

"Zooming out" can eliminate the daily panic and monthly stress. Because if we're going for profit, freedom, and ease, a steady monthly income doesn't get us there.

Think about it this way: if your business relies on *you* showing up to deliver your expertise, and you want to bring in the *same* amount of money every month, that necessarily means you'll have to work with clients about the same number of hours every month. That means working the same number of hours during the holiday months, or months you're on vacation with your family, as you would during months where you aren't.

Not only does that sound hard, but it doesn't even really make sense to try.

What if, instead, you had a financial goal *for the year*, and as long as you hit that goal, it didn't *matter* when you worked with clients?

In theory, this means you could go away for *months* at a time, and still hit your financial goals (assuming your services were priced profitably).

When you're trying to hit monthly goals, it's hard not to feel stressed if you need a week away for spring break with the kids. It's probably why you feel the need to work extra hard before you leave and then after you return—assuming you actually managed to ditch your laptop while away.

What if, instead, you planned your business from the beginning knowing that there'd be some months where you'd make two to four times as much money as you need each month, and other months where you might not make *any* money at all, and *that's actually what you're going for*?

What if you knew that *that* is how you achieve not just the *money* goal, but the lifestyle goal, where you're able to check out when you go on vacation, have a "slow" month, and not have to stress about it?

Can we normalize, and even celebrate, the fact that when

we are our own bosses, selling our expertise, our income is going to ebb and flow? How it's almost impossible for it *not to?*

If you're selling premium services, and you only need 10 to 24 clients a year to hit your goals (because they're paying premium prices), then trying to close those clients on this manufactured one to two clients per month timeline is just unnecessary, not to mention unrealistic. There are too many outside forces at play, the bullseye to hit is just a bit too narrow, and you'll drive yourself crazy.

I always think of the scene at the end of the movie Match Point. It's a movie about love, deceit, and murder (and tennis), but the theme that keeps coming back is that life is full of these tiny chance moments that can fundamentally change the trajectory of your life. In the movie, we see a tennis ball hit the top of the net and bounce up; it could easily fall either way— the match point that determines the winner. There's also a key piece of evidence that's thrown into a river, but, on the way, it taps the railing. In slow motion, the viewer waits in suspense to see which way it'll bounce, deciding the murderer's fate.

I think about that visual a lot, because so often life comes down to that chance. You can do everything right; a client can love you and be ready to hire you, and then something that has nothing to do with you can derail the project.

Something like this happened to Erika Stanley, the brains behind branding agency *MileEndDigital* and artificial intelligence education company *AI Queens*. She was booked out for a solid two months when a client suddenly and unexpectedly needed to postpone their engagement for personal reasons.

Erika was bummed; this meant losing revenue for now, and

possibly forever, since she couldn't count on the client actually coming back. But by that point, she'd gotten used to this process and *annual thinking*, so she wasn't stressed. In fact, she saw this as an opportunity! She tracks her numbers, so she knew that even if this client never came back to her, her goals would still be on track. She decided to reallocate this new chunk of time to working on her podcast.

Unfortunately (and fortunately!), she didn't get the chance. Just a few days later, an old prospect who'd held off on hiring her called to say she was ready. She asked if Erika could squeeze her into the schedule as soon as possible. "Well, yes, I can!" Erika said, and put her into the newly opened slot.

A few days after that, the first client returned. She was dedicated to working with Erika and booked into her *next* open slot three months later. Erika was now booked three months in advance. The postponement of that first client actually led to an even better outcome!

Life won't always deliver some perfect, magical outcome—and that's not the point. Business ebbs and flows, and when you think annually, you give yourself permission to let that be true. A client postponing, going quiet, or even disappearing doesn't suddenly turn your business into a crisis. It's part of the rhythm.

When you expect these fluctuations and plan for them, you stop overreacting to every short-term wobble. Annual thinking shifts your focus from what's happening in the next two weeks to the bigger picture: how many clients you actually need over the course of a year to hit your goals. That perspective alone removes an enormous amount of unnecessary stress. And often, it'll work out in your favor, and you'll be glad you didn't waste all that energy stressing!

This also reminds me of something Seth Godin said when I interviewed him live at one of our in-person retreats in Brooklyn in 2025. I'm paraphrasing, but he essentially said that we often assess our decisions based on *outcomes*—and that's a mistake.

For example, he said, if you buy a lottery ticket and you win, was it a *good* decision to buy the lottery ticket? He would say "no"; buying a lottery ticket is *always* a bad decision because the odds are impossibly against you. If you happen to win, you still made a bad decision. You just got extremely lucky.

Some of our decisions won't yield the outcome we wanted. Does that mean they were bad decisions? That's not how Seth would look at it. We can only make a decision with the information we have at that moment; we can't qualify that decision after the fact once we know the outcome.

So, he concluded, we should focus on just making good decisions, irrespective of the outcome.

I would add that, overall, if we keep our focus on making good decisions and avoid the distractions of fear-based "what ifs", we'll usually come out on top. Maybe not in each decision, but overall.

And it's *always* a good decision to put intentional, consistent effort into marketing our business, filling our pipeline, nurturing our leads, and continuing to develop our skills so we can increase the value we deliver. You may want the outcome to be that you close exactly two clients every month of the year, but that's pretty much out of your control. All you can do is make and act on good decisions that'll make the outcome you want *more likely to happen*.

And the likely outcome of making those good decisions is that, over time, you'll attract and close more and more higher-paying clients, as you get better and better at both the value you offer and the way you run your business.

So what if you focused on the decisions—and stopped putting so much pressure on the outcome?

That's the power of Annual Thinking. It lets your financial goal take shape in dozens of different ways over the course of a year. And it stretches all those "will this client say yes or no?" moments across a longer timeline, which means you're far more likely to hit your goals overall, when any single conversation is, let's be honest, a toss-up.

Annual Thinking, Practically

First, as you learned in Part One, we start with the 50/25/25 Rule to Profit and Freedom to set our Good, Better, and Best annual revenue goals. Once those targets are clear, we reverse-engineer the price points needed to support them. These numbers become the foundation for everything else—where we put our effort, what we do and don't include in our offers, how much we can afford to outsource on each project, and which processes we need to tighten.

If you aren't regularly hitting the price points that support your Good goal, you're still in the startup stage of your business. Your prices aren't supporting your basic lifestyle yet, so you must invest heavily in generating demand and in getting the reps you need to increase the real (and perceived) value of your work.

Getting those reps in is how we were able to raise our 1-day Brandup from $3,000 to $10,000 in under a year. We did dozens of these projects in those early months, which meant we got really good at them. With each one, we learned something new, finessed the process, and looked for ways to add value so the next one was even stronger.

By the time I realized we should raise our prices, we were already wildly underpriced for the demand we'd generated. Were we hustling? Yes. Was that short-term hustle worth it for the knowledge we gained? Absolutely. We hustled hard upfront so we could relax on the backend.

Once we were consistently charging $10,000 for a 1-day and $15,000 for a 2-day, everything shifted. The month-to-month ups and downs no longer mattered. Whether we did two projects, or four, one month and none the next, I wasn't worried. As long as I stuck to a simple marketing rhythm—sending two emails and blog posts a month, attending a few strategic events, and staying genuinely connected to my network—I knew the work would keep coming. Our reputation had taken on a life of its own.

The best part was that every client turned into a referral partner. As we served more and more people, the referrals themselves created a reliable and consistent pipeline.

After that first year, I created what later became the Freedom Calculator based on the 50/25/25 formula (none of these had names at the time; they were simply spreadsheets I used to plan our business and calm my nervous system). That's when

I finally realized we could slow down. We didn't need to take every client the moment they appeared. We no longer had to squeeze clients in. We could schedule projects intentionally and still make room for marketing, creative work, and our next business project, our online course.

This is when I realized I didn't need two projects a month. I needed *sixteen to twenty-four projects a year*, a mix of 1-day and 2-day Brandups. A couple of years later, when those same projects were priced at $25,000 to $35,000, and my annual revenue goal increased to $360,000, I only needed ten to fourteen projects a year. That shift created more and more protected time for authority marketing and for building my second business selling courses. And the more I invested in my authority, the higher the demand grew, and the more confidently I could continue raising our prices.

And throughout the journey, I had to get really comfortable with going for the annual number only. Because when you're selling $35,000 projects, they're not going to come in a steady drip.

And that meant I had to manage my cash flow and my access to capital. Because the key to Annual Thinking is your...

Capital Cushion

You might be wondering how this works in real life. Do you need to be making a lot of money before annual thinking is even possible? How are you supposed to cover your bills right now if your income arrives later in the year?

Annual thinking only works if you can finance the dips. You

can zoom out and plan your year, but your bills still show up every month, even when your revenue does not.

That is why you need a *Capital Cushion*.

Your Capital Cushion is the money that carries you during the stretches when revenue is not arriving on schedule. It gives you stability when business feels slow. It keeps you from taking on nightmare clients or cutting your prices just to survive. It helps you stay committed to your annual plan, even when the month ahead looks thin. And it lets you breathe in the slower seasons or in the months you intentionally take off.

A Capital Cushion is the reason I was able to spend months writing my first book. It gave me the freedom to invest in building our first course and, later, to scale it in 2019, instead of filling my calendar with paying client work. If I had not had that cushion, I would not have had those options available. I would have been forced to take clients and operate entirely at the mercy of my cash flow.

Without a cushion, you are always one unexpected expense or one lost client away from panic mode. With a cushion, you get the time and space to make smart, long-term decisions that support sustainability and growth. You are not pushed into saying yes to work you do not want, or work that will not be profitable, simply because you need cash *today*.

A Capital Cushion gives you leverage.

And here's something that's incredibly annoying: the people who build sustainable freedom-driven businesses aren't necessarily the most talented. They're the ones who buy themselves enough *time* to let their model work. You can be incredible at what you do and still struggle—because running the business *well* matters just as much. The Capital Cushion makes that possible.

How to Build Your Capital Cushion

The Capital Cushion can take different forms depending on your circumstances:

- **Cash reserves.** The simplest option: money in the bank to cover your expenses while you build. Even if you have it, I don't necessarily recommend using it (as I will explain).
- **Cheap or free credit.** A 0% interest card, a line of credit, or access to financing you can pay down quickly once revenue kicks in.
- **Strategic debt.** This is a last resort and I do *not* recommend high-interest debt for more than a couple of months, if you can help it. I'll always recommend looking for low-cost alternatives, and I *never* recommend going into debt for anything frivolous. But used strategically—to build skills, to fund marketing, or to bridge timing gaps—credit can be a powerful resource.

You'll notice two out of three of these are "other people's money," i.e. debt provided by either banks or credit card companies. And all sorts of feelings can get stirred up when we think about debt.

The general consensus amongst most business owners I talk to is that any debt or owing any money, except for maybe a mortgage, is "bad" and should be avoided at all costs. A lot of small businesses refuse to even open credit cards because just having them—without any balance!—is associated with being a delinquent, or immoral, in some way.

Well, I'm gonna say it: I think business owners who avoid credit out of fear are building their business with two hands tied behind their backs.

I've changed a lot of minds on this over the years, and people almost always thank me afterward. So I'm going to be direct. Despite the stigma around credit, it's one of my favorite tools—and one of the most misunderstood. Most people won't even talk about it, much less use it well.

Before that, I want to address this: people's access to capital is wildly unequal. Depending on your background, you may face institutional or personal barriers—from student loans dragging down your credit score, to family members who damaged your credit, to the very real systemic bias certain groups face when applying for financing. If that's you, you may need to build slower. You may need to get creative about reserves. And that's okay.

But I've also met countless people with no systemic obstacles who sabotage themselves with their mindset. They've been indoctrinated to believe that "all debt is bad," so they never touch the tools that could help them stabilize. They refuse to use credit as a bridge and then wonder why they're always stuck in panic mode.

The Capital Cushion strategies I'm about to explain require radical responsibility on your part to learn how to be strategic and logical with money, and to keep emotions out of it. It's not easy, but with practice, this can be an incredibly valuable tool.

This is *not* permission to access credit and then spend it on things that'll never bring money back into your business. So, like, don't open a credit card account, buy a Peloton you'll never use, and claim *I* told you to do it.

If you want to play the long game, you need oxygen. The Capital Cushion is that oxygen—the buffer that lets you make CEO moves instead of desperate ones, and keeps you alive in the dips so the plan can play out.

Here's how you build it:

1. **Know Your Runway.** What does it *actually* cost to keep the lights on each month? Not fancy dinners out, not the "nice-to-haves." I'm talking *bare-bones survival*: rent or mortgage, food, insurance, utilities, childcare. Forget the $7 lattes (or don't if they are a need-to-have for you; it's your life!) Add it all up and multiply the total by 5. That's your *bare minimum* cushion, and you'll want to build a cushion where you have access to at least that much. More is always better.

2. **Build Your Cushion.**

    Got savings? Great, that can be part or all of your cushion. Got a 0% credit card or cheap credit line? Perfect, that buys you time. The only option is high-interest credit? Then listen carefully: use it *only* if you have no other option and you have a plan to pay it down in a couple of months. Otherwise, you're not building a safety net; you're digging a deeper hole.

3. **Fund It on Purpose.** Whether the entire five-month cushion is cash in the bank or access to credit depends on your comfort level. I personally prefer a mixture, be-

cause I don't want five months of cash sitting in a bank account earning less than 4% interest. I'd rather put that cash into investments so that compound interest can work its magic. Growing and maintaining my cushion requires both saving cash and actively opening access to credit to make sure I have sufficient cushion at all times.

I first discovered this strategy back in 2007 when I began working as a real estate agent at 23. The numbers seemed to be in my favor: any apartment I found a renter for would generate a 15% commission on the annual rent, of which I would get 50%. If I rented a $6,500/month apartment, there would be an $11,700 commission, and I would get $5,850. For someone whose biggest payday up until then had been a really good night bartending, where I'd go home at 5am after a thirteen-hour shift with $350 in my pocket and feel like I was on top of the world, that kind of money was another level. And it seemed within reach, if I were to believe the broker that hired me (which I probably shouldn't have!) He said he would train me in the expensive SoHo loft market, where monthly rents ranged from $5,000 to $15,000, and that I would be good at it.

It was time to really bet on myself.

But I wasn't going to try this new venture while still bartending all night. Because I needed to give it everything I had, I was going to have to figure out how to live until I made my first deal. This was the first time I opened an interest-free credit card for $10,000. They gave me six months before the interest would kick in, which to me meant that I had six months to find success.

I lived as cheaply as possible while I hustled my butt off showing apartments. The very first family I showed an apartment to actually said yes—it was a $4,500 place and was going to be an immediate $4,100 payout to me. *This was too easy!*

That's when I learned the hard lesson not to celebrate a deal until the check is cleared. We had all the paperwork; it was a sure thing… until it wasn't. After that deal fell through, I was sad—but I saw hope! I could do this.

But five months later, *I still hadn't closed a single deal*. I was getting close to my $10,000 limit and I was freaking out.

Then in June 2008, just as my deadline was approaching, I closed a $4,200 apartment, followed by a $13,500 apartment, and thus secured two commission checks totalling $15,930.

These numbers are sealed into my memory because I was tracking every dollar so closely back then. I immediately paid off the entire balance and felt immense pride—I had bet on myself, I'd made it happen, I didn't pay any interest on that money, and now I knew I could make a living doing this.

Real estate ultimately didn't work out for me, but it gave me an immense amount of confidence. Not because I was very successful at it—I wasn't—but because it was ridiculously hard and I didn't die doing it. It forced me to put myself out there in ways that were very uncomfortable, meeting strangers to show them apartments I've never seen while making small talk and trying to convince them to say yes when I had zero sales training. Perhaps most importantly (and relevant to the career path I *did* take), it allowed me to develop the conviction to bet on myself, and use other people's money to do it.

I've funded my entire business for the last fifteen years, mostly with credit cards and lines of credit (LOCs), almost entirely using interest-free credit cards. Even now, with cash in the bank, money in investments, and savings in retirement accounts, I continue to use these methods to fund my business. As of this writing, Steve and I collectively have 23 credit cards plus 2 lines of credit. We both have credit scores in the high 700s and rarely pay any interest.

Note: I'm not a financial advisor, and I'm not a billionaire with hacks "only the rich know." I've been tentatively vocal about these financing moves for years because I've been scared of being misinterpreted or even "wrong." What if something about what I'm doing *is* actually irresponsible? Or is there a better way I don't know about? I'd hate to give people bad financial advice or get them into trouble.

But it's worked for me for long enough, and continues to be something I can't find *anyone* talking about in detail.

So I'm going to share how I look at it, and how much it's helped me grow my business. It should go without saying that it's your responsibility to take the advice that's right for you and do only what you can trust yourself to handle. I hope your goal is to build the skills and trust in yourself to use these strategies, rather than assume you can't trust yourself. Consider that my disclaimer.

OK, now for the fun stuff!

Credit is a tool. It's not good or bad, and it carries no moral weight. Yet many people treat any form of debt as a personal failure. Dave Ramsey is a big reason why. His name is so closely associated with debt, and his simple, absolute rules are easy for overwhelmed people to understand.

Yet Ramsey's advice is for people with steady employment and predictable income. And because he doesn't make that distinction explicit, people treat his message as a universal financial truth. Business owners then apply his employee-based framework to entrepreneurship—and that's where it breaks down. Advice designed for salaried stability does not translate well to the risk, timing, and cash-flow realities entrepreneurs face.

Ironically, in a world that treats debt as a moral failing, we also admire massive companies and the people who built them, without acknowledging that almost all of them were built with leverage. In *Shoe Dog: A Memoir by the Creator of Nike*, Phil Knight shares that he was once more than $2 million in debt. At the time, he didn't know he was building Nike. He was simply investing in his business's future. That's how most businesses are built. Any time I invest heavily in my own business, I think about him.

When we ignore the role leverage plays in building real companies, and instead manage our finances like employees because we don't see ourselves as real businesses, we miss a huge opportunity. Ramsey presents his rules as universal, but his advice is not built for entrepreneurs. He assumes people cannot be trusted to make more nuanced financial decisions, such as prioritizing high-interest debt or using credit to create more income. His teachings are aimed at beginners with limited ways to earn more. When entrepreneurs absorb that mindset, it holds them back from the very opportunities that could grow their businesses.

Here's how I think about it: The more access to capital I have, in the form of credit or access to lines of credit, the more space I have to think and act strategically in my business.

It allows me to acquire knowledge and skills more quickly through coaches, programs, and time to learn.

It allows me to test things in my business and in marketing without everything *having* to work perfectly—which is key because not everything *will* work perfectly, ever (thanks, universe!)

But most importantly, it allows me to *breathe from month to month*. As I've become more successful, it allows me to stay on track with my retirement and long-term wealth-building goals rather than dipping into my personal savings and investments when business is slow. It allows me to invest whenever and wherever I need to, never having to wait for a check to clear.

I can't tell you how many people have told me they are ready to invest in learning from us so they can make more money, but they *can't until a client pays them*. It's an exhausting amount of time and energy wasted.

Almost every single one of those 23 credit cards Steve and I own started as a new credit card with 0% interest for 12 to 24 months. I've opened them liberally, especially whenever I have a big investment to make that includes a discount for paying in full. Why would I pay $20,000 for a program over the course of a year when I can open a credit card, pay $16,000 in full, save $4,000, and just pay the card off instead?

Most people don't do it simply because it doesn't feel good to pay $16,000 upfront. It's emotional, not logical.

I also open interest-free credit cards when I want to prepare for big investments coming up. What people don't realize is that the worst time to try to access capital is when you actually need it! Banks don't want to give you a 0% credit card if you owe money or if your credit score is in the tank.

They also won't give you that much if you don't have a credit history, so it's important to *build* your credit history when you can. You do this by having credit available, using it, and paying it off in full and on time every month. The longer you do that, the better your credit score.

This is why I recommend using your credit card to pay for everything—everything that doesn't charge a fee, at least—and then paying the balance off in full each month. If you're already paying for things in cash or with a debit card, this approach shouldn't feel scary. *You're still spending only the money you actually have.* The difference is that you're using your credit card as a pass-through: it functions like a debit card that settles once a month instead of every day, while quietly building your credit score and creditworthiness at the same time.

I am aware that the ultimate winner in this game is the credit card companies. And while I'm not a fan of *this* part of the system, it's the game we're all playing whether we like it or not. So I'd rather play it well—and teach you to do the same—rather than opt out on principle and have my business and mental health suffer. (Plus, when you play the game this way, the credit card companies make ZERO dollars off of you.)

I've had many years to work this muscle. I was privileged to have a dad who thought about this stuff and opened a credit card for me that I used for approved items when I was 13. That means when I was 23, I had *10 years of perfect credit history*—

such a gift! It's why I was able to access $10,000 in free money when I was 23 to give real estate a go.

I realize a lot of people don't have that, but you can get it by *starting right now*. Instead of paying for *anything* with cash, *always* put it on your credit card, and pay the balance in full at the end of the month. You won't pay any interest, and you'll be building your credit score. Open new cards every 6 to 12 months to continue increasing the amount of credit you have available.

Remember, opening a credit card doesn't mean *spending the money*. You don't owe anything by having *access* to the credit. As obvious as that sounds, I have this conversation with business owners all the time. Some people are terrified of opening a credit card because they equate it with debt. A credit card with no balance is just *access to credit*. It's also not debt if you pay the full balance every month. It's only debt once you spend it *and* don't pay it off at the end of the month, and start accruing interest.

The reason we want to open credit cards regularly to build our total access to credit is that when we use credit strategically to build our business, we really don't want to use more than 30% of the total credit we have available. Which means we need access to three times as much credit as we might actually want to use.

Which brings me to…

The 30% Credit Utilization Rule

This rule says you should try to use no more than 30% of your available credit at any given time. Staying under that threshold signals that you can manage credit without relying on it too heavily, which helps protect your credit score. If you go above it, your score may dip because lenders see higher utilization as a sign of financial strain, but that dip is usually temporary and rebounds once you pay down the balance.

This means our goal is to never use more than 30% of our total available credit. Which means, ideally, when you calculate your Capital Cushion, you want 30% of your available credit, plus savings, to cover a five-month runway.

When I see how much credit I have available in total, I instinctively multiply that number by 30%, and *that* number, in my mind, is the amount of credit *truly* available to me.

So if you need $10,000 a month, or about $50,000 runway to cover your business and life (before taxes), what you really want is at least $150,000 in available credit.

And if that sounds unnecessarily large, or even scary, remember that I'm not suggesting you *use* it. If you *do* use it, be strategic about how and pay it off so that you never pay more interest than is absolutely necessary, if any at all.

Imagine you have $100,000 in credit available. You have no balances and a high credit score because you pay your cards in full every month.

Then you hit a couple of slow months, and your cash starts to run low.

You know you'll continue marketing yourself. You're even

going to use this "extra" available time to double down on building your business's value by doing everything I've shared in this book. Maybe you're going to join a community or training program or hire a coach.

So rather than freaking out because your cash cushion is getting low and you're going to have to start using your credit cards without paying off the balance in full, open an interest-free credit card. (Search "best 0% apr credit cards" and NerdWallet will usually come up. Look for the top offers with the longest 0% apr timeline offered, sometimes up to 24 months.)

If you already have $100,000 in available credit and a decent credit score, they'll likely offer you $10,000 to $20,000 with a five-minute application. If they give you $20,000, you just received that money to use *now* for *free*, and saved on the interest you would've had to pay if you started carrying balances on your high-interest cards.

Why *wouldn't* you do that? It's just math!

That said, there's one situation where you shouldn't open a new credit card account: when having access to that money makes you *stop doing the work.*

Use the credit to relieve pressure, and give yourself the space you need if life takes you out for a while. But if the safety net causes you to stop marketing, nurturing your pipeline, or doing revenue-generating work, then you're just accumulating debt with no plan to pay it off. Whenever I take out a 0% card, the date the interest kicks in is burned into my brain. I always plan to pay it off the month before, and if I cannot do it all at once, I pay as much as I possibly can. (Remember, the goal is to pay *no interest. Ever!)*

Some 101 Credit Card Basics I want to make sure you know (because I've met too many people who don't know this, as nobody teaches this stuff, but it's an important part of the story here):

- This bears repeating: when you use a credit card for all your expenses and pay it in full every month without carrying a balance, you're not carrying debt. You are, however, building your *creditworthiness*, as reflected in your credit score.
- You cannot have a good credit score without demonstrating your ability to use credit and pay it off. No credit history means no credit score. Once you open your first credit account (like a secured credit card or student loan), it typically takes three to six months before you'll have your first score. That first number often lands somewhere in the mid-600s range, depending on how you pay it off, but the amount of credit you'll receive will only increase the more you demonstrate creditworthiness.
- Sometimes holding a big balance on a couple of interest-free credit cards can temporarily lower your credit score. While I usually just hold the balance until it's time to pay it off, even when I have the cash (because why pay it off until you need to?), you can also use the cash in your bank account to pay it off in full one month and then start using the credit card again for everything to essentially *pull the cash* back off the card. This will bump your credit score right back up (the mysterious

credit score gods, whoever they are, love to see a big balance get paid off in full!)
- Those 0% balance transfer offers are not as good as they seem because you usually have to pay a 5% fee. If it's available to you, it is better to open a 0% credit card, and "pull the cash" off the card by paying for everything with it, keeping your cash, and using that cash to pay down the high-interest cards instead.

Now let's talk about how to use cash flow to manage your credit cards.

The 3C Boogie: Credit Card Cash Flow Strategy

The 3C Boogie—which stands for Credit Card Cash Flow Boogie—is a way to manage your cash flow when you're carrying credit card balances to minimize, or eliminate, interest expenses, improve your credit score, and maximize your rewards. Once you understand it, it's going to seem totally obvious, but you'd be surprised how many people *do not do it.*

The Problem: The SideStepper

Many people fall into what I call the "SideStepper" pattern when managing credit card debt. Here's how it typically works: They have credit card balances, monthly expenses, and income coming in. They aren't making enough to pay off their credit cards in full, so cash comes in and they use it directly to cover their living expenses. They leave their credit card balances untouched and plan to pay the balances off when they have "extra" money beyond their normal expenses.

Let's say that both credit card balances and monthly expenses are $10,000. When $10,000 in revenue comes in, the SideStepper uses that money to pay those expenses directly, leaving the card balance untouched and only paying the minimum.

The problem? That $10,000 balance keeps accruing interest—often hundreds of dollars a month at typical APRs. High balances also hurt your credit score, especially when your utilization exceeds 30% of your available credit.

The Solution: The 3C Boogie
The 3C Boogie uses logic over emotion. Instead of sidestepping your debt, you create a continuous cycle of payment and usage. The principle is simple: use all incoming cash to pay down your credit card balances (in full if possible), *then* use the card to cover your expenses.

Using the same example:

When $10,000 comes in, you immediately pay off your $10,000 balance. Then you use your credit card to pay your $10,000 in expenses. You're not spending more; you're just changing the order of operations.

Because you paid off the credit card in full, you pay no interest compared to if you "sidestepped" the payments.

People tend to avoid doing this because they're scared of not having any cash. But they *should* be more scared of paying interest unnecessarily!

Of course, this isn't always the case. Sometimes, you don't have enough coming in to pay off the entire balance. That's OK if it's a 0% interest credit card, but if you have a high interest rate, this can get you into trouble—you want to avoid it at all costs.

So, in the same scenario, if the credit card balance is *higher* than the money coming in, you still want to pay the card down as quickly as possible (ideally as soon as the money comes in). This is when the *timing of your payments* matters. Credit card interest is only charged if you leave a balance, but it isn't based on the amount you leave unpaid; it's typically based on your *average daily balance* (or sometimes the sum of the daily interest amount) over the entire previous billing cycle. So if your balance sits at $10,000 for 20 days and you only manage to pay it down to $5,000 for the final 10 days, your interest isn't calculated on the $5,000 left over. It's calculated on the average: (20 days × $10,000 + 10 days × $5,000) ÷ 30 = $8,333. The lower you can get that balance *and the sooner you get it down*, the more days in the billing cycle you're carrying a smaller number, and the less interest you pay. That's why the 3C Boogie works: you're shrinking the balance as early and as often as possible, which drags down the average daily balance and keeps your interest charges to an absolute minimum.

But remember, we don't *ever* want to carry balances on a credit card with an APR. If you plan ahead, build your credit score up, keep accessing more credit whenever you can, and utilize 0% interest credit cards (and, of course, focus on building a profitable business model), then you can largely avoid paying any interest.

Three Benefits of the 3C Boogie

First, as I hope is obvious, you'll save significantly on interest charges. By paying down balances with each cash inflow, you minimize the time that debt accrues interest. In the above scenario, this could save hundreds of dollars in just a few months.

Second, your credit score will improve. Credit scoring models reward regular usage and payment patterns. When you consistently pay down significant portions of your balance, you demonstrate creditworthiness. Additionally, by cycling payments this way, you're more likely to keep your utilization below the crucial 30% threshold that affects credit scores.

Third, you'll maximize rewards and benefits. When you pay expenses with credit cards instead of cash, you earn points, cash back, or travel rewards on every dollar spent. Over time, these can add up to thousands of dollars in value that you'd miss by paying with cash. I haven't paid for an airplane flight or hotel room for my family in years.

How to Implement the 3C Boogie

Successfully implementing the 3C Boogie requires letting go of the emotional weight and any sense of shame associated with debt. Debt doesn't define your worth as a person; it's simply a financial tool to be managed strategically. The key is to look at the numbers without emotion and create a systematic plan.

Start by ensuring your financial records are up to date and accurate, including all balances, interest rates, and credit limits. Then commit to the cycle: cash pays cards, cards pay expenses. Always pay the highest interest credit cards first and in full.

This simple shift in cash flow management can dramatically improve your financial position over time.

But I know these ideas can feel intimidating, especially if you've spent years believing credit is something to avoid.

Take Jess Dyroff and Katie Koch, co-owners of Brightside Creative. They were running a strong business—great clients, solid referrals, increasing demand. And like many small business owners, they secretly held the belief that capital was dangerous, that taking on debt was irresponsible, and that *responsible* business owners only spend what they already have.

They avoided opening new credit cards and hesitated at first to apply for a line of credit when I suggested it. At the same time, even when cash was flowing, they operated with the belief that everything could come to a halt if a couple of clients disappeared at the wrong time.

On one coaching call, I mentioned in passing that Steve and I once carried a total balance of $100,000 across multiple credit cards. Jess practically jolted upright. She'd never heard another business owner talk openly about capital, let alone treat it as normal.

And that's when it clicked for them:

Capital isn't a sign that something is wrong. It's how businesses survive long enough for things to go right.

Around that time, their revenue was strong. Their bank account was full. Even though it felt unnecessary and uncomfortable, they followed my advice and opened a $25,000 line of credit *while things looked good.*

At the time, they could not imagine what they'd ever need it for.

Three months later, August hit.

A few things happened at once. Projects failed to come through, and an unexpected family emergency made full-time focus on the business impossible for a few months. Revenue dipped sharply. It was the exact kind of cash-flow contraction every business eventually experiences—just not on your preferred schedule.

"If we didn't have that line of credit," Jess told me later, "we would've been out of business in August."

Instead of scrambling, delaying payments, or passing their stress onto collaborators, they used their line of credit exactly as intended: as a bridge. They paid their partners on time and kept their commitments. They avoided taking on nightmare projects out of desperation, which would have created a huge burden on top of what they were already dealing with. And they kept showing up for the long-term work that would carry them through the rest of the year.

Here's what was most interesting to me: both Jess and Katie admitted that they *could not have heard this in their first year of working with me.* It immediately sounded unreasonable. But once they had a real business model in place, pricing consistency, and a clear pipeline, capital planning stopped being scary and started being strategic.

They also learned something critical along the way: **you have to access capital *before* you need it.** Banks don't extend credit once things start to look shaky. When business is good, you're creditworthy. When cash gets tight, doors close.

Their story is another example of how annual thinking and the Capital Cushion can give you peace of mind on the wild ride that is being a business owner. You don't build a sustainable, freedom-driven business by timing cash *perfectly*. You build it by giving yourself enough runway to weather the dips and stay in CEO mode. For context, many venture-backed companies expect to operate without profit for 18 to 24 months, with plans to start raising again in 12 to 18 months.

Jess and Katie didn't survive August because they hustled harder. They survived because they finally understood this chapter's core lesson:

It's not how much money you have; it's how confident you are in your ability to make money, paired with how much time you've given yourself to do it.

Shift in Thinking: Build Your Runway

I know I just spent a money mindset chapter talking about credit cards, cash flow, and the 3C Boogie. That might feel unexpected—but it's exactly what you need.

Affirmations won't calm your nervous system when you're starting every month at zero. Mantras won't help when a client postpones and you're wondering how to cover rent. And no amount of "abundance mindset" will fix a business model that keeps you in monthly panic mode. I can't tell you to "think like a CEO" without giving you the actual tools to make that possible in practice.

Real financial security isn't a number in your bank account. It's confidence in your ability to make money, plus enough runway to let your model work.

Annual thinking gives you that runway.

The Capital Cushion gives you breathing room. Together, they free you up to make longer-term decisions and stay focused on the strategic, value-building activities that actually build a sustainable business—instead of running like a lion is chasing you, constantly reacting to whatever showed up (or didn't) in your inbox this week.

It's hard enough to be a business owner selling expertise and wearing all the hats. The No BS Business Model is about cutting away the nonsense that makes it even harder. But we can't just flip a switch. Transitioning to a new model takes time, and you still need to support yourself while you do it. Which means cash flow is a critical piece of the puzzle.

All of this talk about cash, credit, and capital is intended to help you find ease in your business and freedom in your life—so you can stay focused on what truly moves you toward your goals.

Take Action:

1. **What's driving *your* need for "steady" income—actual cash flow problems, or emotional comfort?** If you had five months of expenses covered and just came off of being booked three months out, would you still panic about an "off" month? If yes, your problem isn't the business model—it's the mindset. And that costs you more than any cash flow gap ever will.
2. **Look at your last twelve months of revenue. How lumpy was it—and what would have been different if you'd planned for that from the start?** Did you take a

bad-fit client in a panic during a slow month? Did you say *yes* to scope creep because you were scared to lose the retainer? Moments where you made a different decision than you wanted, out of fear, are moments where Annual Thinking could've helped you make a more strategic long-term decision instead.

3. **If you had a long Capital Cushion right now—cash, credit, or both—what would you do differently in your business tomorrow?** Would you finally raise your prices? Say no to that prospect with the red flags? Invest in the coach or program you've been "waiting" to afford? What's the gap between what you're doing now and what you'd do with a cushion? That's the cost of not building one.

If You Only Take One Thing From This Chapter:

Financial security isn't a number in your bank account. It's confidence in your ability to make money, plus enough runway to let your model work. Stop chasing monthly goals that reset to zero every 30 days. Start thinking annually, build your cushion, and give yourself permission to let revenue be lumpy—because that's how premium businesses actually work.

CONCLUSION

When my son Axl was six and started taking drum lessons every Tuesday, I decided it was the perfect excuse to take up some casual singing lessons, just for fun. Soon after, the school invited me to join their adult band program, an idea I immediately clocked as *something I wouldn't do even if you paid me a million dollars...* because *I cannot sing.*

I'm just a student! I don't even do karaoke! I couldn't possibly sing on a stage, with a band.

They explained that this was *kinda the whole point.* Adults of all skill levels practicing together and performing live at a bar, *purely for fun and with no expectations.* (No expectations? Ha! They didn't know me at all...)

Despite having spoken on lots of stages, the idea of singing in front of *anybody* terrified me.

Yet something in me knew I *needed* to do it.

A few months later, I was headlining the show as the sole vocalist in our band, "Shadow Ban'd." I sang eleven rock songs — including Nirvana, Garbage, The Killers, The Beatles, and Fiona Apple. Singing the songs was fun, but doing it on stage to a room full of strangers was an out-of-body experience. And it was scary as shit.

But I did it... *because* it was scary. I did it because I know that *doing hard things* makes me stronger and more confident.

This philosophy—doing the uncomfortable thing on purpose because of who you become in the process—has shaped my entire life.

In 2019, the organizer of TEDx Colorado Springs reached out after reading my book and invited me to give a TEDx talk. He said it could be on anything, so I hired a coach to try to figure out what the heck I was going to talk about.

We spent three full days walking through every pivotal story from my life, and "doing hard things on purpose" was the theme that kept surfacing. Jumping before you feel ready. Choosing the challenge because of what it demands of you. (My talk ended up being called "When You Bank True Confidence, Anything Is Possible." It's linked on the resources page at scalesolobook.com/resources!)

I'm sharing this at the end of this book because *confidence* is the core ingredient of The No BS Business Model.

And confidence isn't binary. It isn't something you either have or don't have. It's something you build over time, through many experiences, small and large, of leaving your comfort zone.

Building confidence is essential if you're going to show up as the expert, lead your clients, give high-level guidance, and inspire trust.

Having confidence does *not* mean you *never* feel imposter syndrome, or insecure, or scared. Everyone feels these things, *especially* people who are constantly growing themselves and their business.

And it's not *just* about being scared or uncomfortable when there's something you have to do, and doing it anyway. It's *proactively seeking out* opportunities to continually push yourself beyond what's easy or comfortable *because of* the growth and fulfillment on the other side.

When I first started teaching the intensive process, and I'd explain how we built a system where we knew clients would take the work we created with almost no revisions, I needed to quote Spider-Man often:

With great power comes great responsibility.

Once you harness the power of this process, clients entrust you to lead them. They welcome the work you're creating—whatever that work is—with little pushback. You're now completely responsible for giving them the best outcome possible.

And that weight of responsibility *can be crushing.*

Most people assume our process makes everything easier, and in many ways it does. But it's also *harder*, because it requires you to *trust yourself, have conviction in your work, and lead with confidence.*

And that kind of leadership can feel intimidating and scary. If you tend to think clients don't trust you because they just aren't trusting people, odds are it's because you don't trust yourself—and that's coming through loud and clear to them.

This is why so many people default to letting the client lead—it feels safer. If the client makes all the decisions, you're not responsible for the outcome. But giving away leadership is exactly what keeps experts trapped, undercharging, and overwhelmed.

The hardest part of building a business is not the marketing, or even the work itself. The hardest part is the work you do on yourself: building the confidence to charge what you're worth, to stand in your expertise, and to trust your judgment and skills enough to tell a client *they should listen to you.*

And that internal work cannot happen in isolation. You build confidence by *doing*: by being seen, by working with clients, by sharpening your craft, by staying curious, by paying attention to your industry, by trying things and learning as you go.

Confidence comes from action.

And you won't get it right every time! Literally *no one does*. But the more you try, stretch, recover, and keep going, the stronger you get.

One of the most valuable resources I've had in building my business is community. Being around other entrepreneurs who face similar challenges in mindset, confidence, cash flow, sales, and marketing has been invaluable. I cannot imagine building what I've built without those conversations. Without hearing what others were trying, what worked, and what didn't. Without knowing my struggles were normal, and realizing that none of us are alone.

If you're reading this book, I'm guessing you are, like me, fiercely independent. We like doing things ourselves. We trust ourselves more than we trust others.

But today's landscape is moving so fast—technology, marketing, client tastes—that you need people around you who are in the arena, trying things, sharing insights, and staying ahead.

Community doesn't just make you feel less alone. It exposes you to ideas and opportunities you wouldn't even know to look for. I shifted part of my model into a low-cost membership beginning in mid-2025—a pivot I had only landed on because someone in my mastermind, who ran a similar business, shared her experience with me. The whole strategy in my business shifted because of one conversation.

You now have The No BS Business Model that can radically change how you operate and where you focus your energy. My hope is that this simplifies your world, so you stop spreading yourself across dozens of tactics and start focusing on the few things that genuinely matter.

Do fewer things, and do them exceptionally well.

If you want freedom and ease without employees, your numbers have to work. And the numbers work when you serve fewer clients at higher prices. Higher prices come from delivering higher value in less time.

And doing that requires building confidence.

To make this real, you've got to take intentional action—as soon as possible before you get distracted, scared, or busy. Join a program, hire a coach, find accountability. Join communities where people are building the same way you are.

One community I hope you'll check out is No BS. Visit nobsmastery.com to learn how you can join the movement of like-minded business owners who value freedom and ease as much as profit, and who are also installing this model in their businesses with our support.

These folks aren't endlessly chasing more revenue and team or growing for growth's sake. These are people who reinvest their time and money into their families, communities, friends, and missions.

We're an ever-growing group of powerful individuals who make up a significant part of this economy, and my mission is to help more of us thrive. Because when small business owners thrive, they create real value in the world. Not by selling more things that the world doesn't need, but by raising others up. Our businesses create value out of our skills, brains, and effort. That value turns into generosity, presence, impact, and a ripple effect that reaches far beyond our own businesses to our communities, friends, families, and ourselves.

It reminds me of this movie starring Helen Hunt and Haley Joel Osment from 2000 called *Pay It Forward* about a boy who is tasked by his teacher to start a movement to change the world. His idea was simple: the recipient of a favor does a favor for three others rather than paying it back. And it needs to be a favor the recipient cannot complete themselves. Imagine how quickly that would multiply if everyone lived by it.

I love that concept. I practice it whenever I can because I know how it feels when others do it for me. I am not a woo-woo person, but I do believe that when we show up with generosity, it finds its way back to us, if only in the good feelings we feel from having helped others.

That ripple effect brings me to this final story.

In late 2019, I received an email from a woman I didn't know in the Philippines. Her name was Christine, and her family had been hit by several typhoons, and she shared how their home was all but destroyed. She had a young son the same age as Axl, and something about that detail kept me from deleting the email. I was wary at first, but I wrote her back trying to figure out if she was real or if it was a scam. We exchanged many messages, and she started sending me photos and videos of her family and the devastation. I cried looking at the photos of her son especially, and eventually I decided it was clear she and her story were real, and I sent her some money. I even did a small fundraiser for her on Facebook.

But money wasn't going to help her long term, and what I really wanted to help her do was create income for herself. I tried coaching her over email, but it wasn't working. A few months later she wrote again asking for help, with an itemized list of what they needed, and I sent her more money. This happened a few more times over the next few months.

At one point I finally asked her, "What does it cost for your family to live each month?" She sent an itemized list. The total was **$650**.

I remember staring at that number and thinking, *I can help her.*

So I told her, "What if I just hire you for $650 a month?" Steve and I had no employees at the time, and we weren't sure what she could do for us, but that wasn't really the point. I felt compelled to help her. Maybe I was impressed with what a self-starter she was. I loved her attitude. I think I liked how clear and specific she was explaining her situation and detailing her asks. I wanted to help support her family, and I was so grateful that we could. And I figured if we could eventually find tasks she could do, we would send them her way.

We began giving her small administrative tasks here and there—mostly just experiments on instagram that we probably wouldn't have done if we had to do them ourselves because we didn't have the time—which went on for about a year.

Then one day, out of the blue and without me asking, she emailed me a PDF she had designed—of me! She used photos she found online and descriptions of our business. It was beautifully assembled, and I was impressed. I showed it to Steve and he agreed.

That's when things shifted. We saw that she had far more skills than we'd realized and wanted to give her more responsibility and more work.

From there, every time we handed something off, she rose to the challenge. She was always ready to dive into something new and diligent in her communication.

Over six years later, Christine is my longest-running team member and the backbone of my business. She is one of the most reliable, dedicated, hungry-to-learn people I've ever worked with. Her pay is many multiples of what it was, and today both she and her husband Pepe work for me full-time.

I share this story for several reasons. I felt drawn to her because of her determination to take care of her family. She built trust with me through every interaction. Her grit and initiative impressed me immediately. She was willing to take a long shot and email someone half-way across the world, and put herself out there for her kid. I not only really respected that, I felt an immediate kinship. It makes me tear up just thinking about it. Then she consistently showed up and made herself indispensable. She is seriously one of the most badass women I know.

But I also share it because it demonstrates something important: generosity requires stability. I was only able to help her—first personally, and then professionally—because my business was healthy enough for me to do so, because I didn't need anything back. I'd like to think I was rewarded with one of the most reliable, effective, and loyal team members because I was able to give without expectation. That's the kind of generosity I want to have more of in my life. It's something I want to help every business owner I teach cultivate, and something I hope to model for my child.

And the reason I've been able to operate that way is because of the strategies, mindset, and confidence I've shared with you throughout this book.

So whatever and whomever it is that matters most to you, I hope the business model I have shared with you can help you be more generous with them, and give more to them without expectation. I find the more we invest in ourselves and our growth, the more we can give to others.

Margaret Mead famously said, "Never doubt that a small group of thoughtful, committed citizens can change the world; indeed, it's the only thing that ever has." This doesn't always mean changing the world in some grand, abstract sense. Sometimes it means building a business that gives you enough stability to show up generously—for your family, your community, and the people whose lives are shaped by the ripple effects of that choice.

If this book helped you, please share it with someone else who could benefit from implementing this model. My hope is that we can create a powerful ripple effect together.

ACKNOWLEDGEMENTS

To Steve, who's been by my side building this life and business for the last 18 years. Thank you for always believing in me, even when I doubt myself—annoyingly so, because to you it's self-evident. And for using your genius to design, and encourage me to use, such a badass book cover. I love you.

To Axl, my seven-year-old son. You pretend not to care that I'm writing this book, but I know it's sinking in. I started chasing time and freedom before you were even born because I didn't want to have a kid unless I had that freedom. You're the reason I keep pushing—I want you to see that you can do hard, big, important things.

To my parents, who are always there to take Axl on NYC adventures so we can have space to do our work, and keep us fed in our most overwhelming moments. Thank you for always being there for us.

To Priya Malani, who's always been there for me emotionally throughout this process. Thank you for being down for anything—whether it's texting me ten times to remind me to plan my photo shoot because you know I don't want to, or reading my finance chapter in a pinch to make sure it's all kosher. You're always looking out for me, and I'm so lucky to have a friend like you.

To Amanda Dahler and that big, beautiful systems brain of yours. Thank you for always being down to make something insane happen. I cannot believe that while I was writing this book, we migrated from Keap to GoHighLevel… and that's just *one* of the crazy things we did! When we look at each other and say "let's just do it," I feel so lucky to have someone as brilliant and dedicated as you by my side, because we're the only people who can pull that off.

To Christine Catipon, who always brings so much positivity and a can-do attitude to everything you do. A great business cannot run well without someone like you, and I'm grateful you're on our team.

To my team of coaches—Eleanor, Emily, Erika, Fani, Katie, Kelly, and Sara—who keep our community supported and prove what's possible with this model every day. Thank you for lending your stories to this book and for being willing to share yourselves in this way.

To Toni Bache and your brilliant mind that *named this book* off the cuff after I struggled with it for months. I'm so lucky to have you in my corner.

To Christine Moore, who tightened my manuscript in the early stages, thank you for cheering on my ideas from the start and giving me confidence that this was worth reading.

To Brette Goldstein, my fairy-godmother editor. Thank you for believing in me so much that you pushed me to make it the best it could be. I'm so grateful you were willing to find every free minute between all the craziness to help me because you insisted this book needed to be seen by everyone.

To Jesse Sommer, my pinch-hitter editor. Even though my

long-winded, sing-songy ways drive you crazy, thank you for believing in my voice and encouraging me to keep it because that's what's special. You're an anal-retentive editor in the best way, and I appreciate knowing I can always count on you.

To Celi Arias, my coach, who showed me that I built a business model! Thank you for encouraging me to make this pivot and supporting me through my insane timeline. Your strategic brain was core to all of this, and I love that you're always so down for everything, believing we can do it.

To Dusti Arab, who promised we couldn't overwhelm you and has been right so far. Your calmness is deeply appreciated.

And to my No BS community—every single person who has trusted me with your business, your time, and your attention. The work we've done together allowed me to develop these ideas, test them, and prove they work. You paved the way for everyone who will read this book. Thank you for being part of this.

www.ingramcontent.com/pod-product-compliance
Lightning Source LLC
LaVergne TN
LVHW010155070526
838199LV00062B/4376